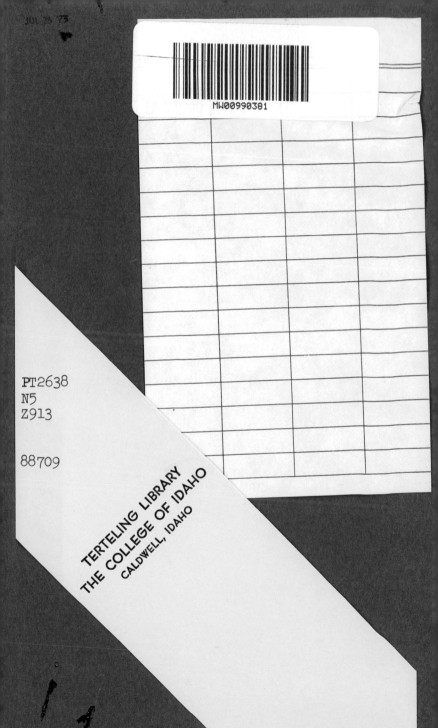

WORLD DRAMATISTS

# ARTHUR SCHNITZLER

REINHARD URBACH

*Translated by Donald Daviau*

WITH HALFTONE ILLUSTRATIONS

FREDERICK UNGAR PUBLISHING CO.
NEW YORK

Translated from the German *Schnitzler*
Published by arrangement with Friedrich Verlag,
Velber, Germany

# CONTENTS

# CHRONOLOGY

| | |
|---|---|
| 1862 | 15 May: Arthur Schnitzler is born in Vienna as the first child of the laryngologist and university professor Dr. Johann Schnitzler (1835–93) and his wife, Louise, born Markbreiter (1840–1911). His first dramatic attempts are at the age of nine. |
| 1871–79 | Attends the Akademisches Gymnasium in Vienna. |
| 1879 | Graduates from the Gymnasium and begins medical school at the University of Vienna. |
| 1885 | Becomes a doctor of medicine. |
| 1885–88 | Is resident at the General Hospital in Vienna. Works in the departments of internal medicine, psychiatry, and dermatology and syphilis. |
| 1886 | Schnitzler begins regular, as opposed to the previous casual, publication of poems and prose in literary journals. |
| 1888 | Travels to London, Paris, and Copenhagen for purposes of study. |
| 1888–91 | Works on *Anatol*. |
| 1888–93 | Works as assistant to his father in the department of nose and throat. He is the coeditor of his father's journal *Klinischer Atlas der Laryngologie* (with M. Hajek; 1891–95). |

| 1889 | Publishes "Über funktionelle Aphonie und ihre Behandlung durch Hypnose und Suggestion," in *Internationale Klinische Rundschau*. |
|---|---|
| 1890 | Schnitzler begins a correspondence and friendship with Hugo von Hofmannsthal, which continues until Hofmannsthal's death on 15 July 1929. Begins correspondence and acquaintance with Felix Salten, which continues until Schnitzler's death. |
| 1891 | Begins friendship and correspondence with Richard Beer-Hofmann and Hermann Bahr. |
| 1893 | Schnitzler's father dies. Arthur enters private practice.<br>14 July: the premiere of the act *A Farewell Supper* from the *Anatol* cycle is given at the Stadttheater, Bad Ischl.<br>1 December: the premiere of *The Fairy Tale* is given at the Deutsches Volkstheater, Vienna. |
| 1894–1927 | Schnitzler carries on correspondence with Georg Brandes until Brandes's death. |
| 1895 | 9 October: the premiere of *Light-O'-Love* is given at the Burgtheater, Vienna, together with the one-act play *Rights of the Soul* by Giuseppe Giacosa. Schnitzler's prose tale *To Die* (concluded 1892) is published. |
| 1895–1912 | Schnitzler has a close, friendly relationship with Otto Brahm until Brahm's death. (Brahm directs the Deutsches Theater, Berlin, until 1904 and the Lessingtheater, Berlin, until 1912 and performs most of Schnitzler's plays.) |
| 1896 | 26 January: first public performance of the act *Ask No Questions and You'll Hear No Stories* from the *Anatol* cycle is given at the Carola Theater, Leipzig (8th matinee of the Leipzig Literary Society).<br>4 February: the first Berlin performance of *Light-O'-Love* is given, together with Hein- |

(1896)     rich von Kleist's *The Broken Jug*, at the Deutsches Theater.

July–August: Schnitzler travels through Scandinavia.

26 July: visits Henrik Ibsen in Oslo.

1 November: the premiere of *Free Game* is given at the Deutsches Theater, Berlin.

1897     23 November–24 February: works on *Hands Around*.

1898     13 January: the premiere of the act *A Christmas Present* from the *Anatol* cycle is given at the Sofiensäle, Vienna.

26 June: the premiere of the act *An Episode* from the *Anatol* cycle is given at the Ibsen-Theater, Leipzig.

26 August: *The Green Cockatoo* is banned by the censor in Berlin.

8 October: *The Legacy* is premiered at the Deutsches Theater, Berlin.

Schnitzler's acquaintance with Jacob Wassermann begins. The novella collection *The Sage's Wife* is published.

1899     1 March: *The Green Cockatoo* is premiered, together with *Paracelsus* and *His Helpmate*, at the Burgtheater, Vienna. *The Green Cockatoo* is given six times in March, then after intervention of the court it is no longer performed (though not banned, it is not "released" to another theater in Vienna).

29 April: the Berlin premiere of *The Green Cockatoo* is given, together with *Paracelsus* and *His Helpmate*, at the Deutsches Theater, Berlin.

1900     Arthur Schnitzler has 200 copies of *Hands Around* printed at his own expense and distributed to friends.

1 December: the premiere of *The Veil of Beatrice* is given at the Lobe Theater, Breslau.

(1900)    (Schlenther, director of the Burgtheater in Vienna, had accepted the play in February, postponed its first performance until June, and in September rejected it. A public protest against Schlenther's action is signed by Hermann Bahr, Julius Bauer, J. J. David, Dr. Robert Hirschfeld, Felix Salten, and Ludwig Speidel.)
25 December: *None but the Brave* (*Leutnant Gustl*) is published in the Christmas edition of the newspaper *Neue Freie Presse*.

1901      *None but the Brave* appears in book edition. Anti-Semitic attacks on Schnitzler appear in the *Reichswehr*. Schnitzler does not respond to the summons of a Court of Honor to answer for writing *None but the Brave* because he does not acknowledge that this council has any jurisdiction in literary matters. (In *None but the Brave* Schnitzler presents a young officer caught in the toils of the dueling ritual.)
14 June: receives the following notification: "The Imperial Army High Command in Vienna by decree of 1 June of last year (Paragraph 646) and on the basis of the decision reached by the local Court of Honor on 26 April 1901, which has found you guilty of insulting the honor of the military, declares you, according to Paragraphs 30 and 33 of the regulations for Courts of Honor, no longer worthy of being an officer in the Imperial Army."
13 October: the act *The Wedding Morning* from the *Anatol* cycle is premiered at Langenbeck-Haus, Berlin (literary evening of the Social-Scientific Association "Herald"). *Berta Garlan*, a prose tale, is published.

1902      4 January: the cycle of one-act plays *Living Hours* is premiered at the Deutsches Theater, Berlin.

(1902)　9 August: Schnitzler's son, Heinrich, is born. 18–20 October: Schnitzler and Otto Brahm visit Gerhart Hauptmann in Agnetendorf, Silesia.

1903　The first public book edition of *Hands Around* is published by the Wiener Verlag.

7 March: the Berlin premiere of *The Veil of Beatrice* takes place at the Deutsches Theater. Schnitzler receives the Eduard von Bauernfeld prize for the cycle *Living Hours*. (Dr. Pattai, a member of the clerical party, formally inquires in parliament why the prize had been given to a Jew. The Minister of Education, Hartel, answers that the judgment had not been made on the basis of baptismal certificates.)

26 August: Arthur Schnitzler marries Olga Gussman, the mother of his son.

12 September: the premiere of *The Puppeteer*, together with Georges Rodenbach's *Le Mirage*, is given at the Deutsches Theater, Berlin.

1904　13 February: *The Lonely Way* is premiered at the Deutsches Theater, Berlin.

16 March: the book edition of *Hands Around* is banned in Germany.

22 November: the premiere of *Gallant Cassian* is given at Max Reinhardt's Kleines Theater, Berlin, in the framework of a "burlesque evening." *The Green Cockatoo* is also performed on the same evening. (A third one-act play, proposed by Schnitzler, *The House Delorme*, had been banned on 19 November by the censor and was never performed or published.)

1905　12 October: the premiere of *Intermezzo* is given at the Vienna Burgtheater.

14 October: the first performance of *The Green Cockatoo* at the Deutsches Volksthe-

(1905)     ater, Vienna, is given together with Kleist's
           *The Broken Jug*. This is the first performance
           in Vienna after the unpleasantness surround-
           ing the six performances in the Burgtheater
           in 1899.

1906       24 February: *The Call of Life* is premiered at
           the Lessingtheater, Berlin. The book edition
           is dedicated to Hermann Bahr.
           16 March: the premiere of *The Big Wurstel
           Puppet Theater* is given at the Lustspielthe-
           ater, Vienna.

1907       *Twilight Souls*, a collection of novellas, is
           published.

1908       15 January: Schnitzler receives the Franz
           Grillparzer Prize for the comedy *Intermezzo*.
           *The Road to the Open*, a novel, is published.

1909       5 January: *Countess Mizzi, or The Family
           Reunion* is premiered at the Deutsches Volks-
           theater, Vienna (given together with *Light-
           O'-Love*).
           13 September: Schnitzler's daughter, Lili, is
           born.
           30 October: the premiere of *Gallant Cassian:
           Singspiel in One Act*, with music by Oskar
           Straus, is given at the Neues Stadttheater in
           Leipzig.

1910       22 January: the premiere of the pantomime
           *The Veil of Pierrette*, with music by Ernst
           von Dohnanyi is given in the Königliches
           Opernhaus in Dresden, and the premiere of
           the opera *Light-O'-Love*, with music by Franz
           Neumann, in Frankfurt on the Main.
           24 November: the premiere of *The Young
           Medardus* is given at the Burgtheater, Vienna.
           3 December: simultaneous premieres are given
           of the *Anatol* cycle at the Lessingtheater in
           Berlin and at the Deutsches Volkstheater in
           Vienna (without the acts *Keepsakes* and *Dying*

(1910)     *Pangs*). The first performance of the cycle, though not complete, had taken place in 1893 in Prague in the Czech language.

1911       14 October: *The Vast Domain* is simultaneously premiered at the following theaters: Lessingtheater, Berlin; Lobe Theater, Breslau; Residenztheater, Munich; Deutsches Schauspielhaus, Hamburg; Deutsches Landestheater, Prague; Altes Stadttheater, Leipzig; Schauburg, Hannover; Stadttheater, Bochum; Burgtheater, Vienna.

1912       In honor of Schnitzler's fiftieth birthday his publisher, S. Fischer in Berlin, publishes his *Collected Works* in two parts: *The Narrative Writings*, in three volumes, and *Works for the Theater*, in four volumes. (The first collected edition of Schnitzler's works, in nine volumes, had appeared between 1903 and 1910 in a Russian translation by B. M. Sablins.)

           13 October: *Hands Around* is premiered in Budapest in the Hungarian language.

           28 November: the premiere of *Professor Bernhardi* is given at the Kleines Theater, in Berlin. On the same evening Otto Brahm dies. The book edition of *Professor Bernhardi* is dedicated to the memory of Max Burckhard, who died earlier in 1912.

1913       *Beatrice*, a prose tale, is published.

1914       22 January: the premiere of the first film made from a text of Schnitzler, *Light-O'-Love*, takes place in Copenhagen under the title "Elskovsleg."

           27 March: Schnitzler receives the Ferdinand Raimund Prize for the dramatic history *The Young Madardus*.

1915       12 October: *Comedies of Words* is premiered simultaneously at the Burgtheater in Vienna,

(1915)    the Hoftheater in Darmstadt, and the Neues
          Theater in Frankfurt on the Main.

1916      15 May: the premiere of the act *Keepsakes*
          from the *Anatol* cycle is given in Volks-
          bildungshaus Wiener Urania, Vienna (on the
          occasion of a charity evening for war relief).

1917      *Dr. Graesler*, a prose tale, is published.
          14 November: *Fink and Fliederbusch* is pre-
          miered at the Deutsches Volkstheater, Vienna.

1918      *Casanova's Homecoming*, a prose tale, is pub-
          lished.
          21 December: the Austrian premiere of *Pro-
          fessor Bernhardi* is given at the Deutches
          Volkstheater, Vienna (the comedy had not
          been permitted to be performed during the
          period of the Hapsburg Monarchy in Aus-
          tria). Schnitzler receives the Vienna Volks-
          theater Prize.

1920      23 March: the premiere of *The Sisters, or
          Casanova at Spa* is given at the Burgtheater,
          Vienna.
          23 December: the German-language premiere
          of the *Hands Around* cycle (the 4th, 5th, and
          6th dialogues had been performed on 25 June
          1903 in Munich) is given at the Kleines Schau-
          spielhaus, Berlin, even though the perfor-
          mance had been forbidden. The erstwhile
          decree was removed on 3 January 1921.

1921      1 February: the Viennese premiere of *Hands
          Around* is given at the Kammerspiele. During
          the performance of *Hands Around* on 17
          February there is a fight in the theater, and
          further performances are banned. After a year
          the ban is removed.
          22 February: tumult at a performance of
          *Hands Around* in the Kleines Schauspielhaus,
          Berlin.
          8 November: a suit is brought against the
          management and the director of the Kleines

(1921)     Schauspielhaus for causing a public scandal with the *Hands Around* performance. The trial ends with an acquittal.

1924     11 October: *Comedy of Seduction* is premiered at the Burgtheater, Vienna. *Fräulein Else*, a prose tale, is published.

1925     *The Judge's Wife*, a prose tale, is published.

1926     *Rhapsody: A Dream Novel*, a prose tale, is published.

1927     *Daybreak*, a prose tale, is published. *Reflections and Aphorisms* and *The Mind in Words and Actions: Preliminary Remarks Concerning Two Diagrams* are published.

1928     26 July: Schnitzler's daughter, Lili, commits suicide.

          The novel *Theresa: The Chronicle of a Woman's Life* is published.

1929     21 December: the premiere of *In the Play of the Summer Breezes* is given at the Deutsches Volkstheater, Vienna.

1931     14 February: the premiere of *The Walk to the Pond* is given at the Burgtheater, Vienna, and directed by Albert Heine. (This play, completed in 1921, had been published in 1926.) *Flight into Darkness, and Other Stories* is published, and the book edition is delivered a day before Schnitzler's death.

          21 October: Arthur Schnitzler dies in Vienna. He is buried at the Vienna Zentralfriedhof in a grave of honor of the Israelite Cultural Committee.

1932     29 March: The one-act plays found in Schnitzler's literary estate—*Anatol's Megalomania*, *Half Past One*, and *The Eccentric*—are premiered. In addition the premiere of the still unpublished one-act plays, *Those Who Glide* and *The Murderess*, is given at the Deutsches Volkstheater, Vienna.

1961–67     A five-volume collected edition of Schnitz-

(1961–67)  ler's works are published by S. Fischer Verlag in Frankfurt.

1969  29 October: *The Word*, a fragment found in Schnitzler's literary estate, is premiered at the Theater in der Josefstadt in Vienna.

1971  19 December: *March of the Shadows*, a fragment, is premiered at the Volkstheater in Vienna.

# INTRODUCTION

When Arthur Schnitzler died on 21 October 1931, a few months before his seventieth birthday, those critics who had jumped to premature conclusions had long since relegated him to those writers who had outlived their reputations. Such commentators were the heralds of an age that despised the past and gave rise to a new man who accepted from the prewar period nothing but the prejudices and resentments that accompanied Arthur Schnitzler beyond the grave. In the leading Nazi organ, *Der Völkische Beobachter* (Munich), there appeared on 27 October 1931 the following statement:

As we have already reported, Arthur Schnitzler, known for his numerous plays (*Anatol, Light-O'-Love, The Green Cockatoo*) and novellas (*None but the Brave, Fräulein Else*), died recently. As a

writer the noted Jewish author had already been
dead for approximately ten to twelve years. The
general public had last heard about him in connection with the scandal surrounding his play
*Hands Around*. Although his death now gives the
so-called major newspapers another opportunity
to publicize their man, the effort to salvage
Schnitzler's fame for the approaching new era,
will most likely prove to be a lost labor of love.
While a master hand at depicting the *süßes Mädel*,
a form of drama which could impress audiences
around 1900, today he is no longer even interesting. Yet, the works of Schnitzler, completely
dominated by erotic effects, were—with the exception of the malicious *Hands Around*—not
without a certain charm, which of course does not
mitigate their inner emptiness. Adolf Bartels desig-
nates Schnitzler as a representative of refined Jewish decadence, and this judgment says basically
everything. Since neither Jewish nor decadent
literary work is suited to the recovering health-
fulness of the German people, Schnitzler's name
will soon be forgotten. For a time people will still
read his novel *The Road to the Open*, which
treats the Jewish question—naturally stopping
short of ultimate honesty.

During his lifetime Schnitzler had been accustomed to such characterizations, as well as to the
envy of his contemporaries who, during the prewar period, had not achieved success equal to that
conceded to him by this anonymous newspaper
report. Schnitzler had to die before the Austrian

essayist Richard von Schaukal, who had learned from Karl Kraus how to be hateful but not how to write with style, could dare to venture forth with his "Postscript to the Viennese Eulogies" (Nachwort zu den Wiener Nachrufen):

> "All Austria mourns for Arthur Schnitzler," asserts the *Neue Freie Presse*, and continues on to elevate to the stature of a creator, poet, and thinker of incomparable importance a writer who, with the help of the "leading" press, made a name for himself forty years ago with the casual products of a physician's idle hours; a writer who, in *Anatol*, a series of light conversations in dramatic form, reproduced a French model in a Jewish-Viennese setting; whose novellas do not surpass the general average of contemporary prose writers; who created several more-or-less cleverly constructed plays; but who, in his more ambitious attempts at historical and didactic drama and in his social novels, gradually became wearying to his regular readers and then failed completely even in his own specialty of providing titillating, erotic entertainment. A number of kindred spirits, second-rate writers and accommodating fellow travelers from the widespread professional circles of non-Jewish journalists, ardently concur with this opinion of the leading papers. ["Arthur Schnitzler und die Seinen." In *Deutsches Volkstum* 14(1932):118.]

In contrast to these anti-Semitic, partisan judgments, in 1931 the critic Herbert Jhering de-

scribed the phenomenon of Schnitzler's diminish-
ing reputation as follows:

> When Schnitzler appeared before the public with
> his first prose works, he confronted that age, his
> age, with the finest, most intellectual perception
> possible. In a masterful manner he portrayed the
> upper-class society of prewar Vienna with its
> skepticism, cleverness, and aimlessness; and in
> portraying this society, Schnitzler dissected it.
> Rarely has the method of portrayal corresponded
> so completely to the subject of the portrayal. In
> this feature lay the inimitable, the unrepeatable
> charm of Schnitzler's works.
> Because this world and the methods used to
> criticize it were identical, the effect of Schnitzler's
> works necessarily diminished after war and rev-
> olution had changed the face of Europe. The
> reason Schnitzler was performed less frequently
> was not because private conflicts had become su-
> perfluous at a time of world upheaval. In the
> period before the war these particular private con-
> flicts were valid and valuable precisely because
> they were characteristic of Vienna and Austria,
> that is, as an expression of their time. Now they
> have lost their representative value and accord-
> ingly have become uninteresting.

Jhering did not note that Schnitzler published
no work that takes place after World War I. The
period from which Schnitzler took his subject matter ended on 1 August 1914, the day that marked
the collapse of the world that he devoted his lifetime to shaping artistically, even after it had long

become the past. Here Jhering should have paid greater heed, for close inspection would have revealed that it was not sentimentality, or yearning for the "good old days," that motivated Schnitzler to create works that were actually histories of a bygone era. And Jhering would have had to ask himself why Schnitzler remained faithful to the same themes and types that had predominated in his early works.

Max Krell has recorded a conversation with Schnitzler in which Schnitzler brushed aside the question of post-World War I Austria and the problems that resulted after the collapse of the Hapsburg monarchy, with the words: "Our generation is hardly able to grasp and certainly cannot shape these events artistically." Thus he gave an answer to the question about the focus of his work: society at the turn of the century belonged to an era that was concluded and could be viewed in its totality. A lifetime would prove insufficient to fathom this world and its people and to portray them in literary terms. Schnitzler's literary estate contains countless plans, sketches, and fragments, which are all variations of the central theme of his production: Vienna around 1900.

Nothing could be more inaccurate, however, than to consider Schnitzler merely the industrious chronicler of his native city at a specific point in time. He did not write documentary histories that merely do justice to the uniqueness of a given situation or event and nothing more. Because Schnitz-

ler gave artistic form to the "private conflicts" of
individuals living at a specific time and place,
these portraits necessarily gained validity as typical expressions of their age. This becomes increasingly clear the further this period recedes into the
past. One may justly apply to Schnitzler what
Egon Friedell says about Henrik Ibsen: "As was
true for Shakespeare, Ibsen will only achieve his
full effect when the clothes of his characters have
become *costumes*."

Arthur Schnitzler lived his entire life in Vienna
and never left the city except for study and vacation trips, lecture tours, and attendance at premieres. Vienna is the center not only of his own
life but of the life of each of his characters. For
Schnitzler, Vienna is the mirror of the world. The
metropolitan atmosphere of the Austro-Hungarian
monarchy lives in his work to a degree that was
not equaled by any other writer at the turn of the
century—neither by Hugo von Hofmannsthal,
whose subject matter carried him into remote dis-
tances of space and time, nor by Hermann Bahr, in
whose "Viennese" plays and novels Vienna was
named as the locale but did not serve an integral
function. In Schnitzler's works Vienna is not a
movable stage prop. This is not true of his other
settings, all of which lack integral necessity, with
one exception—Paris in *The Green Cockatoo*.
Neither the Bologna of the Renaissance nor the
Spa of the Rococo dominates the action of their
respective dramas so completely that *The Veil of*

*Beatrice* could not take place in an Italian city other than Bologna or *The Sisters* in Vienna. Even the unidentifiable castle in *The Walk to the Pond* is situated in an imaginary region of a Danube valley, the Wachau.

Vienna is the center of Schnitzler's world. All travels by his characters and all attempts to flee the inescapable lead back to Vienna, where their destiny is fulfilled. After Schnitzler, only Heimito von Doderer made Vienna so alive in his work—the Vienna of the 1920s—although with different techniques. Doderer recognized the uniqueness of his predecessor:

> Whoever can grasp, shape, and conjure up the aura of a place, its people and things, creates that place, its people and things anew. In this fact lies the historical importance of Arthur Schnitzler, who not only accomplished this achievement with respect to Vienna but—and precisely this point constitutes the historical importance of his deed —was the first to do so.

The Vienna in which Arthur Schnitzler was raised was the Vienna of the expansion years. Five years before his birth, in 1857, Franz Josef had sent his minister the order that the "extension of the inner city of Vienna" be taken in hand at once. The central feature of the reorganization was the Ringstraße, the wide horseshoe-like boulevard lined with public buildings that circles the inner city. While Schnitzler was growing up, the Ringstraße was a gigantic construction site. It was a period of outer calm but of inner tensions that were only barely held in balance. The atmosphere of excitement, threatening upheavals, and intoxicating waltzes made an impression on the young Schnitzler. He experienced the decadence of this Ringstraße era at the race track and on the promenade and was deeply involved with a circle of friends whose harmful influence he recognized but from whom he could only gradually release himself. His growing artistic capability may have contributed to his decision to gain his independence from this group.

In a loose-knit cycle of scenes entitled *Anatol*, Schnitzler portrayed the problematical nature of a life devoted to the often repeated, yet melancholy pleasures of the moment. Although later he scarcely acknowledged this work, it still retains its theatrical effectiveness today because of its accomplished artistic form. The Ringstraße symbolized the life-style of society during the expansion years. Splendor, decoration, and exuberance concealed deception, falseness, and hypocrisy. The Ringstraße is a lie transformed into concrete. It simulated a power the empire had lost and, by donning the masks of past architectural styles, it offered an illusion created out of stone as a reality that people willingly accepted. The paintings of Hans Makart, whose name is used as a label for a style of living and a brief era in the early 1880s, reflected by their suggestiveness and artificiality, the meaningless eroticism and soulless mechanization of instinctive drives that characterized the times.

Behind the decorative facade of official morality the conventions of playacting were established. Role-playing became the life-style of society, not as a theatrical, pathetic, or affectatious exhibition, not as a play before God, but as a game of individuals with each other, everywhere and constantly. In the world of role-playing there are no barriers of class, birth, or wealth. Anyone who wishes may play. Power goes to the most accomplished player. The society of players claims unlimited pleasure in all areas of life, particularly in the erotic. Pleasure is cultivated as a game, with simple rules, refined forms, and complicated consequences. The partners are stripped of their individuality and become types. Affection is replaced by desire, fidelity by flirtation, and marriage by affairs. A life devoted to the moment replaces that devoted to permanence, constant change replaces binding union. There is empty talk instead of genuine conversation, lethargy instead of concentration, stylization instead of naturalness, associations instead of ideas. The player is threatened with the destruction of his illusion from two sides—from without by the intrusion of reality into his fictional world and from within by the realization of his own falseness. In vain the player tries to avoid fate, which may attack him in the form of love, passion, madness, or death (by means of a duel). In a decisive situation the player confronts the truth that he had repudiated.

Not everyone, however, joins in the game. Opposite the players stand others, those who do not know the rules or who cannot play, a situation that provides countless possibilities for conflict. The constellations change but the basis remains: the life of people with one another and against one another is determined by the game. Thanks to the fiction they have created, the players seem to be superior to the nonplayers, who are delivered up unprotected to reality, to truth. They have not been granted the capability of finding refuge in illusion. The "call of life" (which Schnitzler used as the title of one of his plays) reaches them directly.

Whoever wants to exist in society, however, must play a role, and he must play it for life, in the manner of the baroque *theatrum mundi*. At that time God distributed the roles and everyone had to act the part assigned to him. But God no longer directs the play. He is dead. Now the play may be determined by fate or chance, as it is also called. The roles are assigned by society.

The type of person chosen as a model for this role-playing society was the actor, who at the court theater had demonstrated how to express great emotions, how to wear a tuxedo, and how to conduct oneself in social situations. The change in outlook toward the actor is the same as the change that took place in society when the generation that had grown up with the Ringstraße came of age at the turn of the century.

The actor had descended from the stage and performed in the midst of the public that became his great partner. He teaches society how to act so that the performance will appear genuine. He teaches deception. Everyone knows that the actor is performing—when he is on stage. When he employs the same techniques in life, he is no longer acting but deceiving.

The young lover type can choose his role, but he must know how long he can play it. Since his role has an erotic content, age necessarily becomes a problem to such a playactor. When he ages he can no longer sustain his role. He does not gradually grow out of his role but practices it as long as possible. Time stands still until it is too late. There is no gradual transition for the young lover, only a sudden change. Then there is chaos when reality attacks the aging playactor—if he has not previously put aside this role and slipped into another one. The lover Casanova became a secret police agent in Venice and then a writer. There is no better example of changing roles.

The one who knows the secret of role-playing tries to exploit his knowledge of the game by distributing the roles. He is the puppeteer type, who

knows the rules and manipulates people. He believes that he has taken over the function God
once had. But he has no relationship with the people he uses as puppets. The aging puppeteer, who
can no longer participate, must despair. He has
deceived himself about himself. To be sure, he has
made the life of each of the others into a lie—for
all roles are a lie when one plays them in life.
(The conscience operates not according to aesthetic laws but to moral laws.) The puppeteer
himself lives a lie, existing in a perpetual state of
youthful self-deception concerning his omnipo-
tence, which has become impotence.

The clever role-players know that both play and
role are rooted in time, and after a youthful period
of comedies and flirtations they enter marriage.
Even this step, however, provides only an illusion
of security. New games begin. Others, as they
grow older, try to establish a relationship with
their children, whom they suddenly remember.
But since they have lived egotistically and irre-
sponsibly, they cannot claim devotion from anyone.

Thus did Arthur Schnitzler portray the people
of his time. Schnitzler's view of the world as a
theater in secularized form, and no longer as a
world theater with reference to God, is an insight
that he shared with many of his contemporaries.
The actor in every conceivable form and area of
life, as genius and as dilettante, never appeared

more frequently than in Viennese literature at the turn of the century. But not in Bahr, Ferenc Molnár, Raoul Auernheimer, or Felix Salten did the tension between moral necessity and role-playing as an aesthetic life-style find such intensive formulation as in Arthur Schnitzler. From his first to his last dramas he created playacting characters, to whom he posed questions about ego and identity, consciousness and illusion, modesty and vanity, and about time, marriage, and children.

While still in his childhood, Arthur Schnitzler received deep impressions from the world of the theater. His father, a laryngologist, had many actors as patients. The young Schnitzler accompanied his father on his calls and at a young age became conscious of the fame of a Charlotte Wolter or Adolf von Sonnenthal, both of whom were frequent guests at his home. The theater led him to insights that, as he wrote once, were decisive "in developing that basic motif of the intermingling of seriousness and playacting, of life and theater, of truth and mendacity . . . that moved and preoccupied me again and again, beyond any concern for the theater and acting, indeed to a point beyond the realm of art."

Arthur Schnitzler had begun to write at the age of nine, encouraged by his father to keep a travel diary. As a young student he was influenced by his reading of Ludwig Tieck, Karl Immermann, and E. T. A. Hoffmann and wrote dramas in the manner of Franz Grillparzer. One of these early dramas, *Ägidius* (begun in 1878), deserves particular mention because it contains the germ of many of his later themes and ideas. *Anatol*, conceived in the manner of popular French farces, was written in the years from 1888 to 1891 but was rejected by S. Fischer, his later publisher. *The Fairy Tale* was published by Schnitzler in 1891 at his own expense. The critic Paul Goldmann regularly published young Schnitzler's poems and sketches in his journal *An der Schönen blauen Donau.*

Hermann Bahr gathered around him in the Café Griensteidl a circle of young, "modern" writers that has gone into literary history under the name Young Vienna. Though this group lacked any formal organization, lifelong friendships between Schnitzler and Richard Beer-Hofmann and between Schnitzler and Hofmannsthal resulted from this early association. This period was so rich in talented young people and artistic accomplishments that it is scarcely possible now to include them all under one heading. The term Young Vienna is just as inadequate to express the diversity of Beer-Hofmann and Hofmannsthal, Hermann Bahr and Max Burckhard, Karl Kraus and Peter Altenberg, Leopold von Andrian and Felix Dörmann, Raoul Auernheimer and Felix Salten, Richard Specht and Otto Stoessl as the term Jugendstil (the parallel in German-speaking countries to art nouveau) is when applied to the painter Gustav Klimt and the composer Gustav

Mahler, the handicraft artist Koloman Moser and the stage designer Alfred Roller, the architects Otto Wagner and Adolph Loos. Let it suffice to say that all of these men replaced the attitude of sentimentality for the past, which they believed was to be seen in the historical emphasis of the time, with a new conception of art and thus enriched and enlivened Vienna to a degree not achieved since the baroque period.

As a young doctor, Schnitzler also participated in experiments relating to the new field of depth psychology. Despite the fact that laryngology, his specialty, had attracted widespread publicity, and even political interest because of the illness and death in 1888 of the German Emperor Friedrich the III, Schnitzler began hypnotic experiments with patients who suffered from hysterical aphasia. He recognized the importance of depth psychology at approximately the same time as Freud, whose theories he anticipated in his first narrative works. As a result, Freud considered Schnitzler to be his *Doppelgänger*, as he referred to him in a letter of 14 May 1922.

At the University of Vienna Schnitzler encountered the problem of anti-Semitism. In his autobiographical notes he discussed the issue:

> The question was very real at that time for us young people, especially for those of us who were Jews, since anti-Semitism began to flourish and was becoming increasingly virulent in student circles. The German Nationalist fraternities had

begun by expelling all Jews and Jewish descendants from their midst. During the so-called promenade on Saturday mornings and also on the "drinking" evenings, clashes on the open street were not uncommon between the anti-Semitic fraternities and the liberal *Landsmannschaften*. These latter organizations were comprised of students from the same geographical area, a number of which were almost entirely Jewish (at that time there were still no dueling fraternities with an exclusively Jewish membership). Challenges to duels were daily occurrences in lecture halls, corridors, and laboratories. Partly but not entirely because of these circumstances many Jewish students developed into exceptionally skilled and dangerous fencers. Tired of waiting for their opponents' effrontery and insults, they themselves often acted in a provocative manner. Their superiority in dueling, which was becoming increasingly evident and embarrassing, was certainly the main reason for the infamous Waidhofner manifesto, in which the German-Austrian student body declared all Jews once and for all to be incapable of settling insults honorably, i.e., by way of dueling.

This resolution deserves to be recorded here. The wording went as follows: "Every son of a Jewish mother, every human being in whose veins flows Jewish blood, is from birth without honor, devoid of every refined emotion. He cannot distinguish between what is dirty and what is clean. Ethically he is subhuman. Friendship with a Jew is therefore dishonoring; any association with Jews must be avoided. A Jew cannot be insulted; a Jew can therefore not demand satisfaction for suffered insults." This so-to-speak official decree was not made public until several years later; but the spirit out of which it originated and the attitude that it expressed already existed at the beginning of the 1880s, as did also the practical consequences that resulted on both sides. When actual insults had been exchanged and particularly when the honor of officers could not be reconciled with student principles, it was not always possible to observe the Waidhofner edict as strictly as its adherents would have liked; but the spirit of these principles, the idea, if one may call it that, triumphed all along the line, and as one knows, not only along this line. One of the Jewish students who belonged to a German nationalist fraternity before the situation had taken the turn just described was Theodor Herzl. I myself saw him parading around in the ranks of his fraternity brothers with his blue fraternity cap and black cane with the ivory handle on which the FVC (*floreat vivat crescat*) was engraved. That they expelled him from their midst for being Jewish undoubtedly was the initial motivation that transformed the German nationalist student and spokesman in the academic debating hall (where without knowing each other personally, we had stared at each other mockingly one evening at a meeting) into a perhaps more enthusiastic than convinced Zionist, as which he continues to live on in posterity.

Schnitzler never avoided the Jewish problem but always felt himself to be an Austrian writer.

As such he created in his novel *The Road to the Open* (*Der Weg ins Freie*) a lasting monument to the various attitudes and styles of Jewish life in the Vienna of the anti-Semitic mayor Lueger.

In his works Schnitzler always aimed at making man conscious of himself and at healing him through understanding. He never surrendered to cheap effects but always pursued seriously and with ruthless honesty the infinite variations of the great themes: the world as theater and man as actor. This view was confirmed by Robert Musil in one of his diary entries: "The early Schnitzler? He was a moralist; how profound he was is immaterial."

Schnitzler devoted himself exclusively to creating individuals. There are no mass scenes in his works, no use of chorus in his dramas. The phenomenon of the mass is reduced to the typical in the individual. Yet, throughout his portrayals of types his goal remained the individual figure—in its egotism or full devotion, in its insistence on independence or willingness for self-sacrifice, in its truthfulness or mendacity.

His characters always serve his ethical principles, which remain hidden, however, behind a psychological screen. No moralizing finger is pointed obtrusively, with the exception perhaps of a few instances in the early works: the conclusion of *Bertha Garlan* or *The Legacy*, for example. Such directness does not recur in the later works.

Schnitzler's method of character portrayal rec-
onciles the type with the individual. Weaknesses
and vices are revealed more easily and simply in
the type, while crimes appear more as frailties and
weaknesses are made more understandable in the
individual. Understanding makes moralizing difficult, but it becomes increasingly necessary the
more the writer differentiates immorality. The
deeper the psychologist probes and the greater his
insight the harder it becomes for him to establish
or to recognize standards of ethical behavior. By
means of his theoretical typology *The Mind in
Words and Actions: Preliminary Remarks Concerning Two Diagrams* (1972; *Der Geist im Wort
und der Geist in der Tat: Vorläufige Bemerkungen
zu zwei Diagrammen*, 1927) Schnitzler overcame
the bewildering confusion resulting from his technique of creating individualized characters. He
wanted to establish a control system to follow the
main road of the psychological norm, while his
characters stray into side paths, running con-
fusedly until they no longer know how to behave,
until they no longer know even themselves.

Schnitzler modified the individual by the typical. Thus tragicomedies, with individual figures,
and puppet plays, with typical figures, are found
side by side in his works. The schematic is found
next to the particular and determinism next to free
will. Schnitzler succeeded in showing the middle
ground between the two extremes in *Hands*

*Around*, which, viewed in this way, stands at the center of his work. Here the figures are types who, nevertheless, secretly have names. Their behavior is common to all of them, yet each individual is given his own unique manner. For example, not every actress kneels in prayer the way the actress in the eighth scene does, but the typical is the exaggeration of a gesture into a pose.

What other reflective writer so seriously and zealously balanced the typical with the specific and devoted his life to the theory behind this problem without having his work suffer? Schnitzler, on the contrary, by his conscious formulation stamped his work with an unmistakable identity as his creation. No detail in Schnitzler's dramas is ever subject to chance. Details are never introduced meaninglessly for the mere pleasure of creating but always satisfy his three criteria for a work of art: unity, intensity, and continuity. Aesthetic form is in every case subject to the control of ethical consciousness. Never would Schnitzler sacrifice a truth for a catchy formulation or alter a characterization merely for the sake of a beautiful sound. Often enough he portrayed hack writers who preferred glibness to truth, but he himself refused to be dominated by his style.

Two directions stimulate the modern theater: documentary drama and theater of the absurd. The former dispenses with characterization, the latter with reality as control. The stage offers either no invention or pure invention, the factual or the fantastic.

Between these two extremes stands character drama, the aim of which is to recreate man in his multiplicity and reality. The individual character is naturally based on a type but has more dimensions than the type. The type determines the character but does not annul the individuality. Schnitzler's drama is not didactic or thesis drama. "Biased attitudes are always cheap; only the character is valuable," was a notation that Schnitzler made "for further elaboration." The essence of the individual character is to convey a complex picture of man and, by the representation of stupidity and commonness, to direct the spectator toward goodness.

This procedure necessarily determines the methods of interpreting these dramas and performing them on stage. The characters must be treated in juxtaposition, for the dramatic action is developed out of them and not out of hypotheses or ideas. Only through such configurations can Schnitzler's plays be understood.

In 1922 Hofmannsthal wrote about Schnitzler's plays:

> Schnitzler's dramas are consummate works for the theater, designed to captivate, to engross, to entertain, and in an ingenious manner to surprise; they are fully satisfying to the spectator in performance, and yet are capable subsequently of

continuing to preoccupy one's feelings and thoughts; their plot and dialogue mutually reenforce each other, the characters are brilliantly conceived, each lives his own life but nevertheless serves only the totality. When one sees these plays performed, one has the feeling that their creator is at home on the stage and has no other ambition than to produce effective theater.

·    ·

The history of Schnitzler's works on the stage can be divided into three parts: from the first performance in 1893 to Otto Brahm's death in 1912; the period between the world wars; the post-World War II period. The first period stands under the sign of Otto Brahm, who premiered many plays at the Deutsches Theater in Berlin. By this means, Brahm contradicted from the beginning the view that Schnitzler's dramas belonged only in Vienna and could only be performed there.

In the period between the wars, however, most performances of Schnitzler's plays did take place in Vienna, above all in the Burgtheater. These productions were partly under the direction of Franz Herterich and Hans Brahm, a nephew of Otto Brahm, and partly under the supervision of the actors Hugo Thimig, Albert Heine, Max Devrient, and Karl Zeska.

Although after 1945 Schnitzler was represented on the German stage by several plays (particularly *Anatol, Light-O'-Love, The Green Cockatoo,*

*Literature*, and *Professor Bernhardi*), the actual
Schnitzler renaissance began in 1960 when Heinrich Schnitzler directed several of his father's one-
act plays at the Theater in der Josefstadt in Vienna. Heinrich Schnitzler's interpretations have
become a model and have created a Schnitzler
style that unites a precise contouring of the figures
with the appropriate tone in each case, whether it
be ironical, vulgar, casual, or presumptuous.
Schnitzler's dialogues can scarcely be surpassed
from the standpoint of nuances. Every wrong nu-
ance distorts the content of what is said. Schnitzler's dramas live on the stage from the spoken
word. Dialogue, chatting, and conversation form
the main ingredients of the action, in which, however, matters of life and death are decided.

The friendly relationship between Schnitzler
and Otto Brahm was beneficial to Schnitzler's dramatic production. After Brahm's death Schnitzler
could no longer achieve any success in the theater
comparable to that of the dramas produced before
1912. Schnitzler had written dramatic and narrative works at relatively the same pace for two decades. After World War I, however, the narrative
work predominated. Except for *The Big Scene*
from the work *Comedies of Words*, premiered in
1915, almost none of the later dramas survived
their premieres. The dramatic works of the late
period, above all *Comedy of Seduction* and *In the
Play of the Summer Breezes*, are still waiting to be

recognized. After World War I no one wanted to perform Schnitzler any longer because he was considered out of date, at least in Berlin. From 1933 on, performances of his works were not permitted in Germany and Austria. After World War II they could not be performed because the starving postwar public was not receptive to linguistic nuances and psychological complexities. Schnitzler's Vienna has become historical for the theater of today, and only a very small segment of the audience are old enough to remember it. Now our view can be freed from the motifs that are bound to Schnitzler's specific age and penetrate to those that enrich our knowledge of the behavior and conditions of men.

The Viennese writer and critic Friedrich Torberg wrote at the beginning of the Schnitzler renaissance in 1960:

> Occasionally in Schnitzler the critic overfocuses on the costume and is unable to view the entire age, in which the character grew out of the costume. But whoever sees in Arthur Schnitzler only that which is dated in his works is looking at him with old-fashioned eyes. Any attempt to give him a helping hand by "modernizing" the dress would be just as inadmissible and invalid as this approach was in the case of the "Hamlet in Tuxedo" of the 1920s. It is not the dress that has to change but the way of looking at the play. And that seems to be precisely what is getting ready to happen at the present time. [*Forum* VII, pp. 286 ff.]

# EARLY FULL-LENGTH PLAYS

> ## Anatol: A Sequence of Dialogues
>
> A superficial man soon finds something profound.
>
> —JOHANN NESTROY

The cycle of seven loosely connected scenes entitled *Anatol* concerns a young bachelor, Anatol, who in each act experiences a new love affair and discusses it with his friend Max.

Scene 1: *Ask No Questions and You'll Hear No Stories (Die Frage an das Schicksal)*. Anatol possesses the power of hypnosis. He could ask his beloved Cora, who permitted him to hypnotize her, whether she is faithful to him. Yet, he does not ask the question, partly because he persuades himself that he does not want to know the truth, and partly because he is convinced that one cannot know the truth. He considers the question "What is fidelity?" to be just as unanswerable as the question "Are you faithful?" He has hypnotized Cora in vain, for she could have told him "just as well without hypnosis" that she loved him.

Scene 2: *A Christmas Present (Weihnacht-*

*seinkäufe*). Fruitlessly Anatol adores Gabriele, a married woman, an elegant lady of high society. She helps him to select a Christmas present for his *süßes Mädel*, who is waiting for him in the out-skirts and whom he describes as a girl who knows how to love deeply and naively. Gabriele is moved, and she has Anatol bring flowers to the girl from a woman "who perhaps can love just as deeply . . . and who did not have the courage to do so. . . ." (See the account of *Light-O'-Love* for a discussion of the *süßes Mädel*.)

Scene 3: *An Episode* (*Episode*). Anatol asks his friend Max to keep the mementos of his love affairs so that he will not forget. Even at the time, he had regarded his brief relationship with Bianca as a casual interlude. It was his feeling, however, that this episode must have been an unforgettable experience for her. Bianca, the equestrienne, returns to Vienna and visits—Max. She has forgotten Anatol.

Scene 4: *Keepsakes* (*Denksteine*). While Bianca forgot her previous experiences, Anatol forces Emilie to revive her past. He requires her to spread out her past before him in order to cast it away along with the pieces of jewelry that reminded her of the individual episodes. Now he wants to marry her, for, as he will assure us later in *Megalomania*, he creates his own virgins. Yet his transformation of the "fallen woman" into a marriageable one proves to be illusory. Emilie retained two precious stones: the least valuable and the most valuable. The one reminds her of the day on which she became the kind of woman Anatol fell in love with as well as the kind of woman he would not want to marry. The other reminds her of her most profitable adventure. His jealousy and her greed are stronger than all of their protestations of love.

Scene 5: *A Farewell Supper* (*Abschiedssouper*). Anatol does not know how to inform Annie that he no longer loves her but someone else and that they must therefore separate. They had arranged things between them in this way: ". . . right from the beginning . . . as we swore eternal love to each other—Remember, dear Annie, whichever partner one fine day senses that our love is ending will tell the other straight out . . ."

Annie embarrasses Anatol. She beats him to the punch by being the first to confess that she wants to end the relationship. She, too, loves another.

But Anatol is not about to let her get away with this ploy. He claims that he has already deceived her with the other woman! At this news Annie is insulted. She would never have gone that far— that is, she would never have *told* him.

Scene 6: *Dying Pangs* (*Agonie*). Anatol loves Else, a married woman. But the constant circumspection, which they have to maintain because of Else's marriage, destroys his love. He realizes he is not the sole man in her life but only a convenient lover. In spite of the danger involved in the present situation, Else prefers that to fleeing with

Anatol and losing the comfort of her marriage. For Anatol, it is unbearable never to be able to embrace his beloved but always the wife of another man.

Scene 7: *The Wedding Morning* (*Anatols Hochzeitsmorgen*). On the evening before his wedding, Anatol had attended a bachelor party, where he bade farewell to his "sweet, riotous bachelor life." After the party he had gone to a masquerade ball and met Ilona, an actress and former mistress of his. On the morning of Anatol's wedding Max finds the two together in Anatol's apartment. Ilona knows nothing yet of Anatol's impending marriage. When she learns of it from Max, she makes a big, dramatic scene and threatens to go to the wedding herself and expose Anatol. Max is the one who discourages Ilona from carrying out her threat, assuring her that Anatol will return to her sooner or later anyway.

*Anatol's Megalomania* (*Anatols Größenwahn*). Schnitzler had written this scene as an alternative for *The Wedding Morning*. It was not performed or published, however, until after his death.

Years have passed, and Anatol has aged. But he has retained his illusions as well as the awareness that he has illusions. Both aspects of his character are tested when young Annette flirts with him, even though she is having an affair with Flieder, who is very jealous and just as sentimentally inclined as Anatol. Yet Annette cannot take Anatol's emotionalism. Even Berta, who was once Anatol's mistress, had made fun of him during their affair and never took his high-sounding declarations at face value.

> ANATOL: And when we swore eternal love to each other . . . you knew all the time that that actually . . .
> BERTA: Certainly—and you? Were you really intending to marry me?
> ANATOL: But we worshipped each other!
> BERTA: Certainly . . . but that is no cause to lose one's reason! . . .

Anatol drags his illusions and memories of past fantasies along with him—he has nothing else.

Anatol convinces himself that he believes in genuine love, which, however, is only genuine as a game. He does not believe it is a game, although he stages it and actually came to an agreement with Annie, for example, under its terms. He lives in constant self-deception. This is his megalomania.

Anatol accepts as genuine life, what in reality is only genuine as a game.

> ANATOL: . . . Such is life!
> MAX: Oh, . . . I beg your pardon . . . life is not that way!

Anatol deceives himself about the character of the game. Again and again he believes that what he is involved in is a binding relationship—one, however, that would exempt him from any responsibility. His attitude is shown by the way he turns even his wedding into a game for which one must be in the mood. He himself determines the rules, and he prevents the intrusion of reality into the game. Thus he does not question the hypnotized Cora beyond the boundaries of the game as played in the conscious state. Reality would invalidate the rules, for it is part of the game to swear eternal love to each other, a vow that is actually meant only for the moment, without thinking of the future (*Anatol's Megalomania*), of the husband (*Dying Pangs*), or of the past (*Keepsakes*).

Annie observes the rules literally and honorably without deceiving either Anatol or herself. Else transgresses against the sentimentality of Anatol's rules because she views eternal love as a relative matter. Emilie did not take literally Anatol's command to destroy the past. She wanted to preserve in their marriage both her jewelry and the memories that it represents. Berta has seen through Anatol. She is a worthy partner for him, since she knows and observes the rules, but she is superior to Anatol because she never takes the rules seriously (Annie had taken them seriously as long as they concerned her). Anatol acted according to the spirit of the rules and at the same time tried to circumvent them. Nevertheless, he always remains threatened by the destruction of his illusions and he never really lives—that is, except for the moment. His life is superficial and never reaches into the depths, it changes but never develops. Instead of being faithful, Anatol seeks new love affairs. Constant variation of the same theme with ever different partners is intended to suppress inner emptiness, but it cannot eliminate it.

First Anatol exploits his possibilities as a type and then repeats them in the endless emptiness of exhaustion. He undergoes no transformation through his wealth of experiences but remains chained to a round dance of ever the same occurrences. He asserts: "I mastered the art of deriving the most experience from the least number of external events. . . ." But that is not true. In spite of his very great effort (expended on collecting as many mistresses as possible) he gains little because he always experiences only the same thing. What he called multiplicity is only the sameness of superficial repetition. Multiplicity as a profound experience is possible in marriage, as Schnitzler later showed, or in realizing all of the potentialities of a relationship, in the struggle between guilt and responsibility, as expressed by Georg von Wergenthin in Schnitzler's novel *The Road to the Open*. Anatol's life could have taken a decisive turn and his character could have been deepened if he had been confronted by the problem of fatherhood. As it is, however, he remains only clever and superficial. He loves variation because he is indolent, comfort-loving, and incapable of fidelity and permanence.

Anatol does not acknowledge people as individuals but simplifies everyone to a type. He describes his girl in *A Christmas Present* as a *süßes Mädel*, but by contrast he makes Gabriele the self-absorbed elegant lady of society. He typifies and thus practices the very superficiality that he appears to resist.

Schnitzler's structural patterns utilize the parallel concepts of variation and association that represent the way his characters live and think. The theme determines the formal structure. The cycle is a circular form that signifies emptiness. By means of this form Schnitzler not only characterizes his figures but also permits them to unmask themselves.

The favorite mood of superficiality is melancholy, which derives from boredom. Melancholy is the mood of the surface, which conceals the underlying mood of depression that drives one into megalomania. Anatol's characterization of himself as a "frivolous, melancholy person" is not a contradiction, for "frivolous" is the logically consistent complement of "melancholy."

By contrast Max could be described as a reflective skeptic. It has been a technique of drama from the beginning to provide the seducer with a companion who keeps the record, consoles the deceived woman, and creates opportunities. Max, however, is not a servant to Anatol like Leporello, for instance, is to Don Juan, but Anatol's friend and counterpart. He is neither the voice of conscience nor a spokesman for Schnitzler but a corrective for Anatol's errors and foolish behavior. He is never Anatol's rival with women, but neither is he a moralist. Instead, he acts as the instigator for some of Anatol's adventures and remains on his side. His masterpiece, the soothing of Ilona, is a solution in terms of the prevailing rules of the game, one of which is that marriage is no barrier to casual affairs.

Even Ernst L. Offermanns begins the postscript to his 1964 *Anatol* edition with the statement that this cycle consists of a series of loosely connected scenes. It is only the new form that is confusing. But this form is closed and complete in itself. None of the scenes is interchangeable without destroying the logical sequence—which is not determined by the plot. The theme of the variations is Anatol's fate in his relationship to women. Anatol's downward course is shown, from the idyll of the first scene to the dilemma, the barely averted scandal of the last scene, along with the intermediate stages of flirtation, rapture, jealousy, farewell, and agony. The first scene shows that Anatol is still subject to his hypnotic powers. He could penetrate into the depths of a soul, learn the truth, and establish a genuine love. Cora's answer could remove all doubts, and thus there would be no cycle. Because of his fear of the depths, however, Anatol robs himself of the possibility of gaining certainty and consequently initiates the sequence of variations. Cora does not allow him to hypnotize her again. The moment of the height of Anatol's power to free himself from his illusions passes.

Anatol's doubt about Cora's fidelity is confirmed by his own actions in *A Christmas Present*. While he rhapsodizes about his love for his *süßes Mädel*, he woos Gabriele unashamedly and is rejected. Out of the moment of opportunity for fulfillment in *Ask No Questions and You'll Hear No Stories* develops the yearning in the second scene and the remembrance in the third. Anatol's decline begins. In the third scene he has no mistress and begins to survey his past. Then it happens that his former mistress Bianca, who loves too often to be able to experience the uniqueness of true love, confuses him with another lover. The time of love, hope, and belief is past. Anatol's star is sinking. He even wants to marry the "fallen woman" Emilie. She loves him and tells him the truth, but he does not mean everything to her and cannot eradicate her memories. In return for his raising her to his level, she is supposed to make every sacrifice. But he cannot forgive her—Anatol makes no sacrifices. In *An Episode* he is not forsaken, only forgotten. In *Keepsakes* he is still the one who breaks off the affair. Not until *A Farewell Supper* is he forsaken. Annie plays his own game and leaves him. *Dying Pangs* shows the death of the love Anatol had yearned for in *A Christmas Present*. Else takes him only for a lover. *The Wedding Morning* leads close to catastrophe. Ilona finally intends to punish him for what he has done to women. Anatol has made himself vulnerable, and Ilona cleverly knows how to utilize this advantage against him.

Of necessity the games that Anatol plays culminate in an affair with an actress. For Ilona life unexpectedly turns into a stage, the realm in which she is accustomed to dominate. Exaggerations are part of the game: "I have been crying over him for six weeks. . . ." Yet this did not prevent her from going to the masquerade ball where she meets and renews her affair with Anatol. In his apartment Ilona tries to overshadow the others by acting like the mistress of the house. When she is unsuccessful in this role—Anatol and Max cannot enter into the spirit of her performance because they are already committed to another play, Anatol's wedding—she stops acting and makes a real scene. In contrast to Anatol, who lives according to and is dependent upon moods (though he does not act them out, for he cannot render artificial feelings in a genuine manner), Ilona commands the nuances that enable her to make trivialities seem original. She can convey her feelings and emphasize them with gestures. Unlike Anatol, who with all his illusions still preserves his sense of shame, she does not feel embarrassed in front of the public because she is used to performing before an audience.

Ilona is sure of her feelings and her techniques,

for she has tested their effectiveness on the stage. One can doubt her love but not her power of expression. Her outburst is to be taken seriously as a performance, although its effectiveness suffers from lack of truthfulness. And Max explains to her that if she declared her love for Anatol in public and made a scandal of his wedding, she would not only hurt Anatol, but she would also make herself appear "ridiculous" because no one would believe in her love.

At the same time Ilona does not lack grandeur, and during this scene there is truth in what she says. It is not she but Anatol who is lying. It is not she but Anatol who is attempting (unsuccessfully) to dissemble. Her recognition of his behavior causes her outburst. What other possibility does she have except to adopt a pose when the others justify themselves by indulging in windy rhetoric? She takes up the cue for revenge that Max had given to rescue Anatol for the moment, and this provides her with a grand exit. Her actual despair and urge for revenge are not so great, however, that she can resist the temptation to appear grandiose and demonic to herself. Immediately she is attuned to the dramatic possibilities inherent in acting out the emotion of revenge.

Thus the cycle is concluded, but the possibilities for further variations are not yet exhausted. Therefore, Schnitzler offered an alternative to *The Wedding Morning*, which is really a preview of the future showing that the game will continue. His alternative is *Anatol's Megalomania*, which is a retrospective view demonstrating that the game did indeed continue.

Two additional variations to Anatol were found in Schnitzler's literary estate. *The Adventure of His Life (Das Abenteuer seines Lebens*; printed in Ernst L. Offermann's edition, 1964), the earliest scene on the Anatol theme, places Anatol between two women, like Fritz in *Light-O'-Love*. Cora in this early version, however, is not a *süßes Mädel* like Fritz's Christine, but a temperamental, care-free girl, who used to love lieutenants and now loves poets. Gabriele represents for Anatol only a temporary infatuation, not a real affair. Anatol lives in the illusion that both women love him. He loses both when they encounter each other at his home. Now he must find two new girls. But this causes this early Anatol no inner conflict. He is just too happy-go-lucky a person.

More significant is the fragment "Süßes Mädel," which Schnitzler wrote on 15 March 1892, after the cycle had already been completed. Before Anatol leaves to attend a ball, he and his *süßes Mädel*, Fritzi, act out the event that lies before him. He knows what the atmosphere at a ball is like, while she can only imagine. He plays the part of himself, and she plays the part of a socialite who belongs in the world of high society. Even in this rehearsal (which is not even a real rehearsal, since the *süßes mädel* is only filling in for the socialite), ostensible playacting turns into seeming reality. The scene that they are rehearsing threatens to become living reality because the *süßes Mädel* in her role as socialite hears the truth about herself, which makes her forget her role. Anatol, who actually wants to leave her, is distracted, and therefore his performance is genuine: he is supposed to act in a distracted manner, since while at the ball he is ostensibly yearning for his *süßes Mädel*. The fragment breaks off with Fritzi's lament that their relationship is only a game of pretending, that Anatol will never be in earnest.

In *Anatol* Schnitzler adumbrated many themes that were to recur in later works. *Ask No Questions and You'll Hear No Stories* contains in essence the theme of *The Puppeteer*, of assuming the role of destiny, symbolized by the power of hypnosis, which Paracelsus, in the one-act play by that name, also knows how to use. The love triangle that occurs in *Light-O'-Love* is foreshadowed in *A Christmas Present*. The motifs of recollection and egotism are brilliantly varied in *New Year's Eve*. *Keepsakes* treats the problem of the insurmountable past, as does also *The Fairy Tale*, with the difference that in the former play the burden of guilt is accorded to the "fallen woman," whose greed overcomes her pretended love. The thesis of *A Farewell Supper*—that lovers should always be completely truthful to one another—

initiates the conflicts found in *Intermezzo*. The egotistically comfortable behavior of the mistress in *Dying Pangs* is treated again in *The Eccentric*. In the latter play, however, it is not the woman but the man who violates his partner's claims to unqualified devotion. The comic situation in *The Wedding Morning* finds its correspondence in *Literature*, the one-act play from the cycle *Living Hours*, in which a woman about to be married finds herself caught between two men. Finally, Ilona, Schnitzler's first characterization of an actress, was to have many successors.

.    .

The individual scenes constituting *Anatol* each had its premiere singly.

Josef Jarno, director of the Vienna Deutsches Volkstheater, was the first to concern himself with these scenes. In 1922 he recalled this early period. (In his discussion two errors of memory occurred: *A Farewell Supper* was premiered in 1893, and *Ask No Questions and You'll Hear No Stories* in 1896.)

In the year 1890 at the Ischl Summer Theater I staged the premiere of Schnitzler's one-act play *A Farewell Supper*, and in the year 1895 in Berlin, on the occasion of a large soirée at the home of the Berlin attorney, Dr. Greling, at which the whole of literary Berlin was present, a performance of his one-act play *Ask No Question and You'll Hear No Stories*. In both countries these occasions represented the first time that Arthur Schnitzler's works had been performed anywhere. In the year 1898 I met my wife, Hansi Niese, in Berlin and persuaded her to play [Christine in] *Light-O'-Love* and [Annie in] *A Farewell Supper* in a matinee at the Residenz Theater in Berlin. This represented a memorable moment in my wife's career, for actually through the performance of these two female characters she thanks Arthur Schnitzler for her rise to great fame.

*A Christmas Present* was premiered in 1898 in the Sofiensälen in Vienna. *A Farewell Supper* was also given at the same performance. Arthur Schnitzler wrote to Otto Brahm about this performance on 22 January 1898: "It was as if one had locked a canary in a bear cage."

In 1898 *An Episode* had its premiere in Leipzig. *The Wedding Morning* was premiered in 1901. The premier date of *Keepsakes* may be given as 10 January 1916, although Schnitzler had written to Otto Brahm about this work on 4 August 1909: "*Keepsakes*, which I naturally do not like either, has already proved itself on small stages."

At the end of the 1890s the well-known actor Friedrich Mitterwurzer was to have played Anatol under the direction of Oskar Blumenthal at the Lessingtheater in Berlin. The project was not carried out, however, because of Mitterwurzer's death. In addition, on 9 March 1899, *The Wedding Morning* was banned in Berlin by the censor for

ANATOL: A SEQUENCE OF DIALOGUES | 51

moral reasons. Finally, five of the scenes of *Anatol*
were performed together as a cycle on 3 December
1910 in Otto Brahm's Lessingtheater in Berlin and
at the same time at the Vienna Deutsches Volkstheater. In connection with this performance
Brahm wrote to Schnitzler on 24 July 1909:

> I have now read *Anatol* again and would like to
> perform it. I agree with your opinion, that not all
> of the scenes should be included, but I would not
> like to omit *The Wedding Morning*. We need it
> as a conclusion because of its humor. Why do you
> want to eliminate it? Certainly it becomes a little
> too boisterous toward the end where Anatol
> throws on his tuxedo, but otherwise I find it of a
> pleasant insolence. By contrast, *Keepsakes* and *Dy-
> ing Pangs* seem to me to be less effective, and I
> would like to sacrifice them, partly also in order
> not to burden humanity with seven different
> things. I am not worried that this will make the
> evening too short. But I know that it will gain
> in impact.

Schnitzler was often critical of *Anatol*. He found
*The Wedding Morning*, in particular, "objectionable." Not the least important reason for his antip-
athy was that the success of these plays was responsible for the cliché that labeled Schnitzler a
frivolous poet and a *bon vivant*.

In a letter to Brahm of 14 August 1909, Schnitzler expressed this idea about *Anatol*: "A different
kind of theatrical effect could be achieved if one

had all five women [in *Anatol*] played by the same actress. The pleasure in the art of transformation of this one actress would in this case replace the pleasure in the change of performers or, if this actress were a genius, would be able to surpass it." This was once done for a performance in the United States.

In 1932 at the Vienna Deutsches Volkstheater Heinrich Schnitzler directed the alternate scene, *Anatol's Megalomania*, for the first time. The same year the Burgtheater added *Anatol* to its repertory, under the direction of Franz Herterich. The Viennese drama critic Raoul Auernheimer wrote in the *Neue Freie Presse*:

> Before the curtain opens for the first time, [Raoul] Aslan as Anatol is already seated on stage facing partly away from the audience. With a mocking side glance at the public of today, he speaks the prologue in a reverie, as if he were just thinking up his speech. Then the curtain parts, Anatol turns his face to the right, and without getting up or changing his position, he begins to speak to Max, who is sitting diagonally opposite him. This is an attractive idea and one that derives from the material. . . .

After World War II Karl Eidlitz staged *Ask No Questions and You'll Hear No Stories* at the Burgtheater on 7 October 1946. On 13 June 1952 Curd Jürgens, in a presentation of the cycle in the same theater, tried to eliminate all references to the time in which the play was written. Rudolf Holzer, writing about this "experimental production" in the *Presse*, stated that Jürgens had tried "to have these events, which after all are completely real, take place on a transparent, illusionist stage. It is, of course, contrary to Schnitzler's intention but . . . not without a strong illustrative effect."

Ernst Lothar's production in 1960 in the Akademietheater in Vienna had a successful run. Lothar's solution was to put *Anatol's Megalomania* at the beginning and thus to transpose the action into the irrevocable past. This transposition and subjective textural changes, however, met with vigorous objection.

*Anatol* has enjoyed more popularity in the United States than any other of Schnitzler's plays. It has been offered as drama and musical comedy, in small workshops and summer stock as well as on Broadway. Often American directors have produced one *Anatol* episode in combination with one-acters of other playwrights. *A Christmas Present* and *A Farewell Supper*, in particular, have been presented in this way.

*Anatol* was first brought to the American stage in 1912, when Winthrop Ames staged five of the episodes at the Little Theater in New York. In this production, John Barrymore played Anatol. The comedy was received enthusiastically by critics and public alike. Charles Darnton, of the *New York*

*Evening World*, voiced the pleasure of the *Anatol* audience:

> If you have read Schnitzler's "Anatol" dialogues you know how good they are, but until you go to the Little Theater you cannot know how much better they act than read. . . . While this form of entertainment—five separate episodes—must be regarded as an experiment, there is no reason to fear it will not prove popular, for these "Affairs" are decidedly lively and witty. To theatergoers who have reached the age of discretion they are sure to prove delightful.

The *New York Dramatic Mirror* claimed that Anatol was John Barrymore's best role to date—"a lovable scamp who may be unmoral but never immoral."

In 1921 Cecil de Mille produced a film version, "Affairs of Anatol." It owed little more to Schnitzler's cycle than title and core plot.

It was almost twenty years before *Anatol* returned to the New York stage. On 16 January 1931 an adaptation of the Harley Granville-Barker translation opened at the Lyceum Theater. In this version, in which six episodes were presented, the female principal in the episode *Ask No Questions and You'll Hear No Stories* was renamed Hilda. The production was subjected to frequent comparison with its predecessor of 1912—a comparison that was seldom favorable. John Mason Brown, unhappy with the entire production, criticized the unsuccessful attempt to revise Granville-Barker's translation with Broadway lingo. Nor did he have good words for the principal actor, Joseph Schildkraut, whose Anatol was "insensitive to the illusions he seeks to preserve in each new experience. . . ."

In 1946 Mady Christians, star of *I Remember Mama*, directed a production by the Equity Library Theater, which showed, according to one critic, "just how good the theater off Broadway can be." The Directors' Theater presented six of the scenes for an off-Broadway showcase in 1956, in which each scene was developed by a different director. In 1958 Karl Mann and Alex Horn presented the entire seven-scene cycle at the Little Theater in New York, using Karl Zimmerman's translation. Critic Francis Herridge believed this production to have firmly carried out Schnitzler's intentions: "For although the central figure might easily be exaggerated to a ludicrous cartoon, they brought out the man's sensitivity and his anguish. They have given depth to what could be a two-dimensional farce."

In 1961 "The Gay Life," a musical inspired by *Anatol*, was produced by Kermit Bloomgarden at the Shubert Theater in New York. In this production Barbara Cook played Liesl, who finally trapped Anatol into marriage. Except for accusations that the musical "almost smothered the original 1893 work with a fresh story line," the production itself had some success.

## *The Fairy Tale*
(Das Märchen)

*The Fairy Tale* is a drama in three acts concerning the transition to a new outlook on life, specifically to new attitudes of naturalness and emancipation that were developing at the time the play was written. This work retains its importance today not because of its theme of the "fallen woman" but because it demonstrates the enduring power of the past.

The past affects the present, and we cannot escape it. Fedor Denner, a young poet, loves the actress Fanny Theren, but he cannot forget that he is not her first lover. "What was, is! That is the profound meaning of the past." He cannot be deceived by his love and does not pretend even to himself that Fanny's past does not disturb him. To be sure, he is above the prejudice that girls who have a "past" are bad, but he cannot escape the knowledge that Fanny has had previous lovers. He has ventilated the musty rooms of his world with a bold spirit, but he has not abandoned it.

He is incapable of experiencing love in a time-less sense. While Fanny lives in the consciousness of the eternity of love, Fedor interprets this eternity as the moment that passes and is overshadowed by what has been.

Yet Fedor's fate is not the main concern of the drama. Fanny, not Fedor, plays the main role. She is thankful to him for not castigating her, as others have done, because she followed her "natural impulses." He helps her to live freely, that is, to follow her feelings without being bound by the chains of convention that prevail around her. Her career as an actress corresponds to her outlook on life. She must be able to enter fully into her roles. She cannot bring prejudices into her acting if she wants to accomplish an artistic achievement. Because she is an actress and a "fallen woman," she is doubly depraved in the eyes of the petty bourgeoisie and intellectuals, who, moreover, equate the one with the other. Fanny's artistic profession enables her to get over Fedor's failure (which stems from his genuine, though fanatic, devotion to truth). By finally accepting a promising engagement in Saint Petersburg, she resolves the suspense of the third act, which resulted from her repeated refusal of this offer while waiting for Fedor to reach a decision. "She has been restored to goodness through suffering and in the process has become an artist. A noble future is beginning, and we are shown a grandiose perspective. Purified and consoled, we are dismissed" (Hermann Bahr).

The characters of the play are all interconnected and all have a function in the drama. At the same time, unlike the figures in Schnitzler's earlier dramas, here they represent more than themselves. The relationship of two minor figures to Fanny may serve as an example: there is Agathe Müller, the aging actress, and Emmi Werner, the novice who wants to enter the theater.

Emmi is a young bourgeois girl who wants to follow the example of the successful Fanny. She badgers her parents into allowing her to take "elocution lessons," which she considers the first step to success—success with men who hold the title of baron or above. "In any event, I want first to become a great actress . . . I will make my way, and when playing comedy becomes ridiculous for me and I have gathered enough applause and fame— then I will marry a titled gentleman."

To be sure there are those who declare that Emmi's "enthusiasm for art" is "not completely genuine." Emmi is not concerned with art. She is concerned with using this detour through the theater to guarantee the fulfillment of her desire to climb socially. The theater is to serve as a means to an end; she views her future career not only as effortless but enjoyable as well. For this reason she cannot understand Fanny's extreme grief, except as a particularly emotional recitation.

At the other end of the path stands Fanny's older colleague, Agathe, who is experienced but hardly successful. She knows that in the world of the theater one must not be affected by personal matters. For her the world of the theater is a world of independence, of freedom; for Emmi it is a world of erotic wishes and dreams; for Fanny it is a world that causes rejection, a world by which one is condemned to unhappiness. Agathe and Emmi fail to see the tormented person in Fanny. Nevertheless, they are both related to her. For Agathe, Fanny represents her lost youth, for Emmi her future success. She is praised in retrospect by Agathe, while Emmi regards her as a model.

While Agathe acknowledges Fanny's accomplishment, Emmi flatters her. Emmi stands enthusiastically on the threshold of the theater world, but Agathe has become indifferent, beyond all feelings of rivalry or competitive envy. As part of this world Fanny is torn between her art and her love for Fedor. The desire for adventure attracts Emmi to the theater. The desire for variety motivated Agathe's theatrical career. Fanny is prepared to leave the stage, although through love she has now become more mature in her art. She must, like Agathe, first experience rejection in order to find her direction. By this process she finally comes to acknowledge the theater as her world. Here she can find her way to self-acceptance, freed from the obligation of despising herself as prescribed by the bourgeois world.

The dialogue in *The Fairy Tale* is cleverly constructed, but it is not always successful because, although it was not Schnitzler's intention, the characters are actually discussing and interpreting themselves.

The drama was modeled on illustrious forerunners: theoretically on Friedrich Hebbel (the inescapable consequences of an act), abstractly on Ibsen (Fedor's hatred of the hypocrisy of life), and practically on the French writer Henri Murger (the life of the petty bourgeois artist).

． ．

*The Fairy Tale* was given its first performance at the Deutsches Volkstheater in Vienna on 1 December 1893. Concerning this production of the play, which he later described in 1912 as "a very respectable play," Schnitzler wrote on 12 June 1894 to Georg Brandes:

> It has been performed in Vienna, in the Deutsches Volkstheater. The first two acts found favor, but the third act failed so completely that it ruined the effect of the entire play. In particular, the audience seems to have found little edification concerning the moral qualities of the play. One critic called to me: "Decency, please." Another spoke pointedly about the "truly frightening moral depravity," to which the play bore witness. A Berlin theater that had already accepted *The Fairy Tale* withdrew from its contract because of this failure in Vienna, and thus I can probably consider the stage career of this play as finished.

Subsequently, however, the play was performed often and successfully in Russia. It appeared on 15

June 1912 in the framework of a Schnitzler cycle at
the Deutsches Theater in Prague under the direction of Heinrich Teweles. Noteworthy also is a
television presentation that was given in Hamburg
in 1966.

## *Light-O'-Love*
(Liebelei)

     Schnitzler's next play, *Light-O'-Love*, a
drama in three acts, also reminds one of Murger's
sketches "Scènes de la vie de bohème." Although
the young people in *Light-O'-Love* are not artists
and the action is concentrated in two couples,
Christine and Mizi bring to mind Murger's Mimi
and Musette. Christine and Mizi represent two
different variations of the *süßes Mädel* type.
Judged in external terms, the circumstances of
each girl's life are similar, but they experience
them differently.

The *süßes Mädel* type may be described as a
loving and frivolous young thing from the outskirts
who, during the flower of her youth, seeks pleasur-
able experience with the young men of better so-

cial class and then, in maturity, marries a workman
—a good man. The *süßes Mädel* brought unappre-
ciated fame to Schnitzler: ". . . if one had the
choice between being 'unrecognized' or 'falsely
recognized'? Of course the latter happens to one
after the seventeenth or twenty-eighth play rather
than after the first, and it is more difficult to re-
cover from," he wrote in a recently published letter, which he had written on 24 January 1908 to
Marie Herzfeld. This type is not as uniform in
Schnitzler as is commonly believed. There are
naive (Cora in *Anatol*), wise, fickle, and corrupt
variations—the latter appears in *Hands Around*,
the only play in which Schnitzler actually names
the character "Süßes Mädel," rather than having
another of the characters simply refer to her as
such. Schnitzler's reaction to the fact that all his
young girls were labeled as *süßes Mädel* is reflected in the words of the puppet Liesl in the burlesque *The Big Wurstel Puppet Theater*:

> Just because I am a single girl,
> And Vienna's the scene of the plot,
> They call me "süßes Mädel,"
> Whether I am or not.

The *süßes Mädel* type can be found as early as
Nestroy, in his *Mädl aus der Vorstadt* (Girl from
the Outskirts). The carefree young people and the
sweet young thing, who is pursued by dandies, appear in this farce of 1845. Nestroy modeled his

seamstresses (Schnitzler's Mizi Schlager in *Light-O'-Love* is a milliner) on the pattern of French grisettes, and it is not far from French *vaudeville* via Murger to Schnitzler. Moreover, there are the variations of the type of *süßes Mädel* found in Berlin in the works of Theodor Fontane and Georg Hermann—not to mention Ernst Wolzogen, in whose works the actual term *süßes Mädel* appears for the first time. One should not, then, give Schnitzler sole credit for creating as a literary type the kind of girl that is spawned by urban life, and furthermore a type that he varied and portrayed ironically, without anyone noticing it.

Once the term was in vogue, all of Schnitzler's female characters were called *süße Mädeln* if they were unmarried. Schnitzler drafted an "Anti-critique" but did not publish it. In it he speaks about *Liebelei* being used as a catchword and about *Anatol*, to whom all subsequent lovers in his works, including Sala, Medardus, Hofreiter, and later even Bernhardi, were compared as "aging Anatols."

> In a completely similar manner the same thing happened with another figure, or let me first say, with the words *süßes Mädel*, that appeared for the first time in a little scene entitled *The Christmas Present*, which was published in the *Frankfurter Zeitung* on Christmas Day 1891. The type to which these words refer surely did not signify anything new, not even in strictly literary terms.

It is possible that by giving certain individualizing nuances to particular characters, to whom this designation is rightly or wrongly applied, I created the impression of greater naturalness and liveliness. What would remain completely baffling, however, if one didn't have to reckon continually with the intellectual laziness and maliciousness of a certain type of critic, is the circumstance that ever since (I mean ever since the designation *süßes Mädel* gained a place in the German language), scarcely a work of mine has appeared in which the *süßes Mädel* is not immediately recognized with shouts of joy among the characters. For this recognition it is only necessary that the character be unmarried. Their other qualities and destinies are not taken into consideration in the slightest, and not only Mizi, who, after all, may claim a well accredited right to this pet name or nickname, but also Johanna Wegrat in *The Lonely Way*, Anna Rosner in *The Road to the Open* and indeed (one might not consider it possible) even Princess Helene in *The Young Medardus* have all been greeted as *süßes Mädeln*. Thus, just as the masculine world is divided into Anatols and homosexuals, the feminine world consists of *süße Mädeln* and married women—it goes without saying, only when my works are being considered. If some of my works had appeared under a pseudonym, even the most perceptive reviewers would have failed to detect what now seems to be so clearly evident, namely, the relationship of my masculine and feminine characters to those prototypes, who were introduced to the public for the first time two decades ago. Moreover, if one remembers now that all of the relationships that exist between my characters of different sexes are designated once and for all as *Liebeleien* [flirtations], one can gain an idea of just how weak-minded, shallow critics have made it easy for themselves, by describing, with the help of words that I must take partial blame for making popular, the truly not inconsiderable variety of characters and destinies that I have portrayed, as merely a constant repetition of the same theme.

At the beginning of this "Anticritique," which must have been written about the year 1911, stands the passage about *Liebelei* being a catchword:

Fairly near the beginning of my literary career I wrote a play in which I portrayed the love of an ordinary young girl for a student from a well-to-do home, showing the happiness, suffering, and death of this young girl. Since the young man is still entangled in a previous love affair, and thus at first takes his relationship with this young girl all too lightly, I named this play *Liebelei*, giving it an overtone of painful irony that can scarcely be missed. More seriously and with equal justification, although of course with somewhat less taste, I could have called the play "Christine's Great Love." The possibility of misunderstanding the exceedingly simple plot is completely out of the question, even for the most limited reader or spectator. This has not prevented a majority of the critics, however, from pretending to construe the word *Liebelei* strictly in its original meaning and acting as if they believed that my play did not concern any profound and strong feelings but merely involved a casual, frivolous escapade.

These comments of Schnitzler should suffice to indicate how he wanted his play understood. As was the case with almost every one of his dramas, Schnitzler worked on *Light-O'-Love* for several years and wrote several versions. Lengthy segments of a folk play in eight scenes exist in his literary estate. The first scene was published in 1903 in a volume honoring Ferdinand von Saar's seventieth birthday. Schnitzler distanced himself from this work, as it were, by noting: "Only to comply with a friendly wish of Mr. Richard Specht do I make this manuscript available to him for publication in this volume." And yet, it is a scene that is complete in itself and that perhaps could even be performed. In a dancing school with its oppressively restrictive and formal environment, two couples meet for the first time. Against this unpromising background evolves a tender, fervent relationship. In this version Fritz and Theodor are not only characterized by opposing qualities— seriousness versus the carefree, melancholy versus frivolity—but also the basic distinction between the two, which lies in the depth of character of the one and the superficiality of the other, is clearly evident. In contrast to the completed version, in this early version Christine also has a past affair to forget. Thus, the uniqueness of Christine's and Fritz's love as the central idea of the play was not yet present in the folk play.

The plot of the final version: By means of an affair with Christine, a girl from the outskirts,

Theodor wants to distract his friend Fritz from his passion for a married woman, a relationship that inhibits Fritz's freedom and that is threatening to become dangerous. But the husband challenges and shoots Fritz just as Fritz was becoming conscious of his love for Christine, to whom he had come to mean everything and who knew nothing about his affair, duel, and death. What she had taken seriously all along, he had only valued as a noncommittal game.

Fritz Lobheimer feels guilty toward Christine. He has deceived her and, without suffering a bad conscience at the time, has told her nothing about his life and problems. Nevertheless, within its fixed boundaries, his relationship to her was genuine. He simply left out his real life and did not bring it along into the game. His conscience and feelings of regret awaken in him when he senses that more than a game could have developed from this relationship. At their last meeting before the duel, Fritz realizes that he has deceived Christine by not telling her the whole truth. Deception occurs at the point where one begins to feel bound or wishes to be bound, where he begins to feel a sense of responsibility. While Fritz has unconsciously played a game with Christine, Theodor and Mizi act by mutual agreement, for they are fully aware of how their relationship will end. Fritz and Christine are more sentimental and romantic. They do not speak as candidly about the past and the future as the other two, who can do so because they

only want to enjoy the moment. Both Theodor and
Mizi know the rules of the game, but Fritz never
lets Christine know that he is acting according to
these rules. The affair is tragic, therefore, because
Christine regards as deception what he intended as
a game. She does not believe in the "repeatability
of the unrepeatable." The game, on the other hand,
is repeatable—it is based on the principle of repeatability. This discrepancy must of necessity drive
Christine to despair. Fritz has experienced the two
types of the social game of love: an affair with a
married woman and an affair with one of those
"girls whom one does not marry" (the title of a
collection of tales by Raoul Auernheimer). As long
as the rules of the game are observed, and people
do not deceive each other but tell the truth, the
game is genuine. Fritz, however, is not capable of
honest, casual, temporary relationships such as
Theodor engages in; thus, even his passion for the
married woman has become a lie. Hermann Bahr
summarized the importance of this for Christine:
"Because he dies of a lie, she realizes that she has
lived on a lie."

While nothing could distract Christine from her
devotedness, she was only a diversion for Fritz, not
the meaning of his life. When she learns of his
death, her life loses its meaning and she rushes off.
Where does she go? To her death, the critics maintain in a rare display of unanimity. Even Schnitzler
in the above cited "Anticritique" speaks of the

"end" of Christine. Yet, he did not venture to express this conclusion explicitly in the drama. Her death is one, but not the only, possibility. Her father, old Weiring, believes with certainty that she will not return, but Schnitzler was honest enough to doubt her death. It would have been easy to show her death unambiguously, as Schnitzler did in *Free Game*, and as he avoided doing in *The Legacy* (in striking parallel to *Light-O'-Love*). With Christine's departure, however, the play is at an end; what will follow is left to the imagination of the spectator.

In 1897 Otto Stoessl, in his "Wiener Brief" (published in the *Neue Deutsche Rundschau*, Vol. 8, p. 205), described *Light-O'-Love* as a play about Vienna: "What gives this first work its emotional content other than the strong play of opposites? This naive, guileless, affectionate Christine with her completely unbroken, simple soul clings to an artful, sophisticated young man. The result is, perhaps more than one would like to believe, a 'Viennese' play; it contains very clearly, beautifully, and distinctly the nature of this city and its barbarity, which to be sure also has a certain charm."

. .

*Light-O'-Love* is one of Schnitzler's most performed plays. The premiere took place on 9 October 1895 at the Burgtheater in Vienna, and the play remained in the repertory until 15 September

1910. In Berlin, Otto Brahm directed the play on 4 February 1896.

On 1 March 1918 *Light-O'-Love* was revived by the Burgtheater under the direction of Max Devrient. This production was performed in different theaters until 10 October 1930.

Then in 1946 the Vienna Burgtheater again produced *Light-O'-Love* together with *A Christmas Present* from the *Anatol* cycle. With reference to this performance Rudolf Holzer wrote in the *Wiener Zeitung* on 13 March 1946 that beginning the program with *A Christmas Present* "produced the truly curious effect of a humorous prologue to the following tragic *Light-O'-Love*." In his opinion, however, the public remained indifferent: "The generation of today has experienced too much that is difficult, frightful, and shattering, to be able to empathize with the resentment toward life of a Fritz Lobheimer or the love tragedy of a Christine." Nevertheless, the play had a successful run from 9 March 1946 until 21 September 1946.

On the occasion of a new production on 12 June 1954 O. M. Fontana wrote: "Conditions change but not hearts." Under the direction of Ernst Lothar the main roles were performed by two well-known actors, Hans Moser and Inge Conradi. The spoken version of their unforgettable portrayals was made into a recording under the direction of Heinrich Schnitzler. *Light-O'-Love* found its place in the repertory of large theaters even in the 1960s.

In 1968 it was performed, with staging by Heinrich Schnitzler, at the Theater in der Josefstadt.

*Light-O'-Love* enjoyed a brief period of popularity among Americans in the early 1900s. Under the title *Flirtation*, it was produced by the Progressive Stage Society in 1905 at the Berkeley Lyceum Theater in New York. In 1907, as *The Reckoning*, it was presented again at the Berkeley Lyceum. This second version was revived the following year.

## *Free Game*
(Freiwild)

In this three-act play the designation "free game" applies to two groups of people: actresses and those who refuse to duel. Schnitzler brought together both themes in one plot and without reservation included this drama in the 1912 edition of his collected works, noting: "A play without great merit, but nevertheless a respectable work for the theater!"

Anna Riedel, a young actress in the summer theater, and her friend Paul Rönning, who is convalescing in the same resort town, are the victims.

The hunters are the military officers stationed in the small town. First Lieutenant Karinsky pursues Anna. He is rejected by her, and when he quarrels with Paul, he is slapped by the latter. Karinsky challenges Paul, who, scarcely recovered from his injuries, has no desire to expose himself anew to the danger of death and therefore is not prepared to duel. Karinsky considers his honor insulted and shoots Paul down. Anna is left with no way out of her dilemma. She has lost her rescuer as well as the possibility of returning to the theater.

The military officers are masters over the destinies of the resort's residents, particularly over the actresses of the summer theater, whose profession makes them popular companions. The actresses are expected not only to serve as objects of society's "games" but also to participate actively. Any girl who refuses to cooperate cannot hold her position for long. She will have everyone against her, especially the director, who has come to a tacit agreement with the public, and who is well aware that he can hold his audience only if the girls of his "art institute" also provide companionship after the performance. The actresses must demonstrate their adaptability in order to remain in the theater. The more compliant they are, the more popular they become, resulting in commensurately greater income as well as increased favor in the eyes of the director. That the girls are ruined in the process is interpreted by outsiders as an indication that they were seeking this fate.

The officers are indifferent to the particular play being performed in the Wurstl Theater. "All that matters is which girls are performing," and for these they have "plans." The girls have to assure their success on the stage by the way they act in private. There is no closed season for "free game." Becoming a "fallen woman" is part of the profession. Their careers as actresses depend upon this condition. Only the girls who fall, will rise. There is nothing paradoxical about the summer theater as an institution. It is clearly a pleasure establishment, which even in its theatrical offerings is geared to the sensuality of the public. The comedy consists of flirtation with the public. The operetta turns into a revue in which even the masculine roles are "all performed by women," the ballet turns into an exhibition, and the costumes into tights. The director turns out to be a procurer. The performance serves the sole purpose of arousing the sensuality of the audience in preparation for the following rendezvous with the actresses.

The scene of the action, which characterizes the double function of the summer theater, is not the theater itself but the square in front of it. Here, with the box office in full view, is the meeting place of sauntering officers and flirtatious coquettes. The impression must not be created that all actresses are "free game." The professional survival of the actresses Fischer and Schütz indicate the opposite. Pepi Fischer, especially, is far from being prey. (The soubrette Fischer is the only living character in the play. Some of the others are only present to discuss the ramifications of the duel, while the remaining characters are stereotyped figures: the director of a second-rate theater, the vain lover, the all-too-ready second ingénue, the overly indulgent cashier, and the profoundly sad clown, who, obsessed by Pagliacci-like jealousy and despair, sees through the activity of this theater.)

The summer theater, which had long been the unrestricted amusement center of bored soldiers and merry actresses, now becomes problematic for the first time because of Anna Riedel. Her refusal to dine with the officers suddenly exposes what the summer theater is and how it differs from the kind of artistic institute that Anna had undoubtedly expected when she accepted this engagement. She was completely unsuspecting about the customs and expectations of the theater world at its lowest social level. Anna does not fit into this world, whose unwritten social laws she did not know. She learns them now but is not able to subject herself to them, although she knows that she will have to conform if she wishes to remain: "If one is pursued for a long time, one finally becomes tired! . . . They consider it sheer presumptuousness on my part that I have no desire to sell myself." Paul Rönning, who wants to free her from this dilemma, is himself destroyed in the attempt.

In an answer to a "Questionnaire Concerning

Dueling" (Rundfrage über das Duell), which was found in his literary estate, Schnitzler discusses theoretically the complex problem that he dramatized in *Free Game*:

> The play does not concern the duel but the obligation to fight a duel. And to be sure not the obvious obligation, which would be a relatively simple matter to overcome, but the multiple forms of the unspoken, secretive, dangerous obligation that is built into our social fabric. . . . Here it happens every day that people unintentionally encounter circles in which the prevailing views necessarily include the obligation to duel. As long as people who decline a challenge to duel are considered cowardly and as long as people feel defamed by the reproach of so-called cowardice, then the obligation to duel will continue to exist. No legal decree, no law will have the power to protect anyone who has insulted another person either actually or in the sense of the prevailing social view from receiving a slap in the face. And as long as this slap retains the symbolic significance that society now attaches to it, no legal decree will be powerful enough to make the person who has been slapped believe that his honor has been avenged or that the individual who struck him is sufficiently punished by a fine of five to a hundred Gulden or even by spending twenty-four hours under arrest. Consequently, when all other means fail, the slap, in all social circles where it serves as a symbol, will signify an absolute obligation to duel.

*Free Game* concerns the real consequences of symbolic acts. As one character states: "The slap, however, does not signify a slap but a mortal insult, as you very well know. What would happen to me in the duel would not *mean* something but would *be* something. . . . And that is an essential distinction."

Social premises have changed today. The dueling question and the operation of a summer theater as a bordello are no longer typical issues. Nevertheless, these themes provided Schnitzler with the opportunity to demonstrate the conflict between the social code of honor and rational behavior, between social determinism and free will. Therein lies the timeless significance of this drama, which Schnitzler himself did not hold in the highest esteem.

•    •

*Free Game* was the success of the seasons from 1896 to 1898. Otto Brahm gave the premiere at the Deutsches Theater in Berlin on 1 November 1896. The censor had objected only *pro forma* to the words of one of the characters, Vogel: "If now the girls from the theater also want to be respectable, one will never know where one is."

On 27 November 1897 the play was performed for the first time in Prague and, on 1 February 1898, for the first time in Vienna at the Carl-Theater.

## Hands Around
(Reigen)

She said to herself, Sleep with him, yes—
but no intimacy, please!
                                    —KARL KRAUS

In the ten scenes of *Hands Around*, the prostitute and the soldier, the soldier and the maid, the maid and the young gentleman, the young gentleman and the young lady, the young lady and her husband, the husband and the *süßes Mädel*, the *süßes Mädel* and the poet, the poet and the actress, the actress and the count, the count and the prostitute of the first scene, meet one another, perform the sex act, and separate.

It might appear to be a risky undertaking to write about *Hands Around*. Indeed, if the main subject were *what* happens, there would be little occasion to devote many words to it. But the only important matter is *how* Arthur Schnitzler has given artistic form to these situations, which are all similar in goal but different in approach.

Since Schnitzler knew only too well that this play would be a source of misunderstanding, he withheld it for a long time, making it available, in a private edition in 1900, only to his friends and other understanding people. How right he was to exercise such caution was demonstrated in 1921 by a trial in Berlin involving *Hands Around*. Nevertheless, even exoneration in the courts never managed to put an end to the scandalous gossip about *Hands Around*.

The ten scenes are actually ten dialogues, which are among the best works in this form ever written in the German language. Arthur Schnitzler achieved the perfect verbal expression necessary to present the most intimate and indiscreet details in the most discreet and at the same time most revealing manner. From the time that he completed these dialogues, Schnitzler had to be counted among the masters of world literature. One cannot marvel enough at his mastery in these dialogues. To exhaust their profundities is impossible.

These dialogues consist of simple conversational exchanges, which, from scene to scene, take on greater significance. The characters talk without really conversing. With varying degrees of eloquence, in which elements of brutality, sentimentality, lust, and flirtation are combined, the mute sex act is prepared for and concluded, Schnitzler conveys the inexpressible (the underlying sensuality) by language. It is the language that unmasks the hypocrisy of the speakers. None of the characters is honest, for each one must prevent the new partner in his second scene from learning about the partner in his first scene (even the prostitute

tries to create the illusion of exclusivity). Everyone plays the game by dissembling, remonstrating,
and expressing seeming reservations, but such protestations are never serious, for they are contradicted by the second scene.

No one is faithful to anyone else—otherwise the
"round dance" (the *Reigen*) would not be possible.
Everyone is consciously unfaithful; not even the
husband and wife assure each other of their fidelity.

The individuals who form the various couples
find their way to each other according to the rules
of society, which has made multiple possibilities
available: dances, parks, inns with *chambre sepa-
rée*, hotel and brothel, casual affairs and marriage.
Everything serves only one purpose.

There is no need for the partners to feel a mutual bond. Except for sex there is nothing between
the couples. These people sleep with one another,
but they do not become intimate. They remain
lonely even when they are not alone. Yet, this loneliness is not man's fate but his guilt. It derives from
lies and deception, lust and superficiality. The
chain is the appropriate form to represent these
variations of unsatisfied lust. Link fits into link, but
the same uniformity, the same varied repetition
always remains. There is no possibility of development, for the meetings cross but never run parallel.

In Gero von Wilpert's *Deutsches Dichterlexikon*
(1963) the section devoted to Schnitzler contains
the statement: "The satirical dialogues of *Hands*

*Around*, with their cynical diagnosis of instinctive life, brought the author *succès de scandale*." But it is not instinctive life that is diagnosed here. Rather it is the behavior leading to the satisfaction of desire that is analyzed. The characters are not types, but their behavior, which is representative of their instinctive life, is typical for the condition or position in which they find themselves. *The* prostitute does not behave in this way, but *a* prostitute can do so. Individual eccentricities and occasional malicious tricks, all of which have psychological causes, make the characters unmistakably different from one another. They are not completely determined by the type, even though they remain embodied in it. The general characteristics that are shared in common by all variations of the type appear in the individual without completely dominating him. Schnitzler succeeded here in unifying the type and the individual. He does not typify the character and thus make him shallow—that would mean to kill something living—but rather the type is individualized, life is breathed into the pattern. Everyone can be this way—for thus is the one, who serves as the representative of all.

Each character does justice to his "profession," for he does not forget his work or his responsibilities because of the encounter. The husband never forgets his business dealings, the poet never forgets his writing, the actress never forgets her roles, and the wife is mindful of her obligation to have children.

No link in this chain is interchangeable with another without destroying the unity of the entire sequence. The cycle is complete in itself. Nothing in *Hands Around* is accidental or reversible. The sequence of scenes cannot be altered. Every figure stands in the place that has been assigned to him or her not only by the social order that forms the basis of the play, but also by the intellectual and psychological structure that endows this sequence of scenes with its uniqueness. In ascending progression the action proceeds from the crude, uncouth forms of love to naiveté and yielding, to the pedantic fulfillment of duty and the search for variety, to intellectual forms of realized experience, to feigned and hysterical sensuality, and finally to refinement and jadedness. From unconscious instinct, through desire for adventure, to game and seduction—to insensibility.

Society is completely represented, except for one type, the elegant lady of high society. But as we already know from *The Christmas Present* in the *Anatol* cycle, she does not enter into the "round dance."

At the beginning there is brutality and vitality. Both disappear, and in the young gentleman they already have changed into sentimentality and nervousness. In the married man and the *süßes Mädel* these qualities turn into shameless naturalness, languid and comfortable. The actress, like the prostitute in the first scene, takes the initiative. In her case, the refined game returns to the realm of the vulgar found at the beginning. The maid and the *süßes Mädel* are alike in their submissiveness; both come from the same social class, only the *süßes Mädel* is a luxury item, a product of society, raised to be a plaything.

The rising and falling line of men corresponds to the circular configurations represented by the women: the soldier who merely follows his natural instincts, the curious, lascivious young gentleman, the domineering, moralizing philistine, the vain intellectual, and finally, as representative of the highest social class, the passively decadent aristocrat, the awkward and effeminate count. The men are distinguished from one another also by their manner of expression, which, however, is distorted and devoid of meaning: the young gentleman tells stories, the husband lectures, the poet reflects, the count philosophizes.

The poet and the count represent the intellectual and aristocratic center of society. The actress seduces and confuses the one with her lack of logic and the other through her disregard of the etiquette of flirtation. She never knows what she wants, only that she wants precisely that man who happens to be in her vicinity—and he is made to realize that it is a special distinction to be chosen by her. For her, man is not an individual but a "principle," even though he scrupulously insists on being called by his name. *Hands Around* leads us from the simple to the extreme and the eccentric, as represented by the actress. The elaborate gestures as well as the small embarrassments, coquetry, and apparent naiveté, all of which normally create emotional intensification on the stage, produce an exaggerated effect here. Conflicting expressions follow each other in quick succession, and she makes no statement that she does not later contradict. She is affectionate and angry, flattering and mocking, all at the same time. Her mouth runs over, but her heart is not full.

This shows the actress's superiority, for her speech flows easily while the poet can only stammer and the count reflect. She, with her common sense, repudiates their empty phraseology about love and the soul as well as their pose of indecision. Yet, as much as this repudiation is justified, just as little can she herself bear even a hint of criticism, unless it is veiled in a cover of flattering words. Demonic pretense and childish behavior intermingle and harden into pose. Of all the figures in the play she is the most difficult to characterize precisely. She changes from moment to moment and hence cannot be defined by any single opinion that she expresses. In both of Schnitzler's great cycles, *Anatol* and *Hands Around*, there is an actress at the end (since technically the last scene of *Hands Around* concludes the circle with characters who were introduced earlier). The actress is the prima donna of a play-acting society, superior to all others because of the advantage she gains from her acting ability.

*Hands Around* uses the form of the medieval

dance of death. The thought of death is omnipresent for the characters and lures them to enjoy the pleasures of the moment. The prostitute says to the soldier: "Come on, stay with me now. Who knows whether we will still be alive tomorrow." And the young gentleman to the young lady: "Life is so empty, so worthless—and then—so short, so horribly short!" In the last scene the count remarks to himself: "Sleep also makes people equal, it seems to me—just like its brother, Death. . . ."

. .

When asked for his opinion of the cycle *Hands Around* the philosopher Georg Simmel wrote on 22 April 1914:

> After lengthy consideration I cannot make up my mind to speak out for the release of Schnitzler's *Hands Around*. My reason for not taking a position is not to be found in the work itself. In it I see the human tragedy—but no trace of lasciviousness or inartistic titillation. But our public is absolutely not mature enough for such a work. The overwhelming majority would read the book only for pornographic interest.

The misunderstandings Schnitzler had to suffer throughout his life reached a high point when *Hands Around* was introduced to the German-speaking public. The history of the performance of this play is connected with scandals. Sponsored demonstrations disturbed the premiere performances in Vienna and Berlin in 1920 and 1921. In Berlin the play was involved in a court trial that lasted from 5 to 12 November 1921 and that ended with the exoneration of the accused directors of the Kleines Schauspielhause. On 2 February 1921 Arthur Schnitzler had written to the famous actress Tilla Durieux:

> It is no secret that I have doubted for a long time, not whether *Hands Around* is an immoral work, but whether it belongs on the stage. Even today I still do not believe that the problems of staging have been solved; everything else that is still being said today against the performances of *Hands Around* is, as far as I am concerned, not discussible.

Nevertheless, on 25 January 1922 Schnitzler went to the effort of outlining a refutation of specific points of the accusations against his play, but he did not publish his statement:

> On the occasion of the performances of *Hands Around*, several new errors have been added to the critic's usual dogmas, to the mistaken views that one critic echoes after the other, as I have discussed previously. One such dogma runs as follows: that one should no longer permit a play to be performed as soon as the suspicion is confirmed that the public, or a greater part of the public, is not attending the performances exclusively for artistic reasons. The second, that it does

not accord with the honor of one's status to accept royalties if these royalties derive largely from people who have viewed the play not exclusively for artistic reasons. The critics will reply: "Dogmas? But have we ever asserted anything of the kind?"

Quite right. Actually, such views were never before, or at least never before so decisively, expressed until the precise occasion of the *Hands Around* performances. I mean only that if these dogmas were based on correct premises, then one would presumably have to apply them generally and not permit them to be directed specifically at *Hands Around*.

Let us proceed logically for once.

In general we judge plays according to whether they are artistically good or bad, whether they are performable or not performable, whether they are theatrically effective or ineffective, and also according to whether they are moral or not.

These, therefore, would be questions that are to be asked in conjunction with every work and that, indeed, have already often been raised. They have scarcely ever unleashed such a hostile dispute, however, as has arisen in connection with *Hands Around*.

What are the causes of this and how does *Hands Around* actually differ from all other so-called plays that have previously been performed on stage?

My reply to these questions is: 1. That in *Hands Around* sexual intercourse is put on the stage. 2. That this situation occurs ten times in succession. 3. Further, that this happens without visible indignation on the author's part. 4. That the play does not concern true love, that is, the kind of love, apparently, that has marital procreation of children as its purpose; finally, that the people who engage in intercourse know each other only casually or not at all, indeed, as is also claimed, do not even know each other by name (which was hardly my intention), and that actually only a purely sexual relationship exists between them.

To begin with the first point: What is the truth of the claim that sexual intercourse is brought on the stage in *Hands Around*? This claim is simply untrue, since at the crucial moment either the stage is darkened or the curtain falls, a technique already used in numerous earlier plays for a similar purpose, as is well-known. To be sure the curtain usually falls for a longer time and is not, as in *Hands Around*, raised again immediately, as soon as the sex act is completed, and that is probably what has aroused the most objection.

We know that on stage very frequently a kiss or an embrace takes place, so-to-speak as a symbolic substitute for the actual sex act, and we have accustomed ourselves to accept this as thoroughly permissible and reconcilable with our artistic and moral principles. It would be impossible to enumerate all the scenes in which a dramatist actually means by a kiss something other than the kiss itself. It would be impossible to enumerate all those conclusions of acts that indicate what must happen, in the context of the play, as soon as the curtain falls. Likewise there are numerous instances where, in the context of the play, the curtain is raised immediately after an embrace has taken place between the two people on the stage ("It is the nightingale and not the lark"). Now either this is objectionable or it is not objectionable. It is not clear, however, why it should be objectionable in one case and not in another. Moreover, it is particularly incomprehensible why it should have the effect of being sensually arousing or morally corrupting when the play concerned is artistically inferior rather than artistically worthwhile. Rather, the opposite is the case, and no one will deny that for people who are so disposed, the sight of Romeo tearing himself away from Juliet is capable of arousing precisely the same feelings as, for example, the moment when the husband in the *Cabinet Particulière* of the Café Riedhof says to himself "What kind of person is this actually" (who has just become my mistress).

One will object, what blasphemy, to compare the chaste love drama of Shakespeare with that artistically inferior scene. Now I am at the precise point where I want to have you. If it is a question of artistic merit, let us speak exclusively about that. If *Hands Around* is an artistically inferior work, then naturally one should not be allowed to perform it, precisely because it is artistically inferior. For those other qualities you have criticized in it are shared with a hundred others, with significant as well as insignificant plays, with works that have a directly moral tendency as well as with works that actually have no other intention except to stimulate the senses and produce a lascivious effect. And again and again, from whatever perspective we try to resolve the problem, the question will always be raised: Is the play concerned a serious literary work or not? . . .

Following the summary of his views in "Concluding Theses," Schnitzler's 23rd and final point reads:

> All of the objections that have been raised against the performance of *Hands Around*, even if they were justified as such, would have to be raised against a multitude of others.

Schnitzler continued to believe that *Hands Around* could be performed. But because he doubted the possibility of finding the artistic discretion and delicacy that every performance would have to demonstrate, he prohibited any further production of this work. This ban is still in effect today.

Before he banned all performances of *Hands Around*, however, Schnitzler had already parted with certain French rights. The result is that *Hands Around* can be legally presented the world over in one of its two French film versions, both called "La Ronde." The first version, directed by Max Ophuls in 1950, is probably the better known. According to the critic Eric Bentley, however, the world was unfortunate in the 1950s in being permitted to see the film while being forbidden to see the play. "Production of the play is, at this point, morally desirable—as a corrective to the distortions which the director Max Ophuls has imposed on the film." In his *Dramatic Event* (1954), Bentley accused Ophuls of "betraying his author by removing the style and meaning."

> [*Hands Around*] embodies a keen sense of life as
> both tragic and comic; life in *La Ronde* is never
> more than a moment of pathos, a moment of ab-
> surdity, a juicy incident, a passing titillation, sour
> romance, wry farce. . . . Schnitzler's serious sad-
> ness has sunk to a cheap cynicism. . . . he [Ophuls]
> has converted a satire into the thing satirized.

Roger Vadim directed the second film version in
1964. Jean Anouilh wrote the script and dated the
last scene as taking place on 1 August 1914, the day
of the outbreak of World War I, which brought an
end to Schnitzler's world. Vadim cast his wife, Jane
Fonda, in the principal role. When the film was
shown to New Yorkers in 1965, in a dubbed version
entitled "Circle of Love," Eugene Archer of the
*New York Times* called it an "ineptly acted vul-
garization of a distinguished play."

In spite of Heinrich Schnitzler's efforts to follow
his father's wishes and keep the play off the boards,
*Hands Around* has found its way to the American
stage in a number of adaptations. Shortly after Eric
Bentley bemoaned the fact that American audiences
were allowed only a distorted version of this work
in Ophul's film, Bentley's own adaptation, also
called *La Ronde*, was produced by the Circle in
the Square in the summer of 1955. Although not always in agreement on the quality of the production,
the critics were more favorable to the stage version
than to the earlier film version. Lewis Funke noted,
in the *New York Times*, the play's "sardonic, piti-

less and penetrating" study of the human animal.

> Schnitzler cut the details fine, unmasked all the little vanities and the foibles, and with a physician's cold approach took no moral position. Still, even he could not refrain once or twice from feeling the pangs of sadness over the whole masquerade. If an audience comes away with a sense of the emptiness of mere physical love, it may be that the good doctor so intended.

While Funke, however, was of the opinion that José Quintero's "deft and understanding" direction trapped and distilled the essence of the play, the *New York Herald Tribune* critic, Paul V. Beckley, hardly agreed with him:

> Too frequently any sense of reality slips off to one side and the performance becomes no more than a series of piquant incidents. . . . [Schnitzler's] point was essentially that one element, at least, cut across all class and social lines. It was, in a sense, a somewhat brittle laughter at the expense of social pretentions in the society Schnitzler knew.
>
> In this version there is altogether too much attention directed to the amusing superficialities and very little to the underlying point the playwright was trying to make. . . . the trouble is simply that Mr. Quintero failed to realize in this instance the essence of the thing.

A second adaptation of *Hands Around* was presented in spring 1960 at the Theater Marquee in

New York. Again entitled *La Ronde*, this version was directed by Patricia Newhall. The translation, by Miss Newhall and Hans Weigert, bore the brunt of Walter Kerr's criticism—"at times it is seriously non-Viennese . . . and at times it is vaudeville-careless."

In 1969 a small, new company produced *Hands Around* as a musical, "Rondelay," in New York. The production was a failure in almost every respect. Clive Barnes, comparing the new musical with the original play as translated by Eric Bentley, accused Jerry Douglas (book and lyrics) of having "gone at [the play's] charms with a meat ax," misunderstanding and misinterpreting Schnitzler throughout. Even the music was undistinguished, a conveyance for the words. "Rondelay" closed after only six performances.

*The Legacy*
(Das Vermächtnis)

*The Legacy* is a three-act drama about the hypocrisy of bourgeois morality, whose representatives value propriety more than morality.

The fatally injured son of a good bourgeois family confesses to his parents before his death that for some time he has been living with a girl who has had a child by him. He begs his parents to take mother and child into their home. The parents respect the relationship of the son as his legacy. Yet they will not let Toni, the young mother, forget that she is not part of the family but is dependent on them. When the child dies, there is no longer any necessity to shelter Toni. She flees from the house and perhaps from life. The death of the child appears to have released the family from its promise. Toni's departure again makes clear on which side the guilt lies. The father comments on other events that have occurred: "One sees now what happens when one once overlooks certain things and associates with creatures who—do not belong to us! What does one get for it in the end? Nothing but scandal." There is no lack in the play of devil's advocates and accusers. The dialogue is often stilted.

Schnitzler wrote to Georg Brandes on 12 January 1899 about *The Legacy*: "As long as the main character is on stage I do not like the play. I find that she has remained quite impersonal. During the rehearsals many ideas occurred to me by which I could have brought the play to a higher level; above all I would have had to keep the child alive." And in 1912, while looking through the works that were being considered for the first collected edition, he noted: "A rather unenjoyable play."

. .

*The Legacy* was premiered on 8 November 1898 by Otto Brahm at the Deutsches Theater in Berlin. On 30 November 1898 the Viennese premiere followed at the Burgtheater.

The public saw in this drama the propagandizing of the idea of free love. Max Burckhard's colorful description of the Berlin premiere (he had marked the play for future use during the period of his directorship, which ended with the season of 1897–98) will make clear the effect on the public at that time:

> In a certain sense this drama is a didactic play. The dramatist has not openly expressed the moral, he has only raised a corner of the covering under which it lies. But the public has not let itself be deceived, least of all the students in the gallery. At the conclusion of the play, those in the upper galleries jubilantly tore away the covering so that free love was presented in a completely stripped state to the respectable, upper-class audience sitting in the boxes and orchestra. "Marriage is after all only an incidental formality, and intercourse between man and woman without marriage is no sin." That is the thesis.

In this 1931 production of *Anatol* at the Lyceum
Theater in New York City, HILDA (Dennie Moore)
is shown with a dumbfounded ANATOL (Joseph
Schildkraut) and his companion, MAX (Walter Con-
nolly).

GABRIELE (Paula Wessely) helps ANATOL (Robert Lindner) select a Christmas present for his *süßes Mädel* in this 1960 production of *Anatol* at the Akademietheater in Vienna. The play was directed by Ernst Lothar.

BARBARA PFLAUM

ANATOL (Walter Chiari) and LIESL (Barbara Cook) in a scene from the 1961 musical comedy "The Gay Life," based on *Anatol*. Kermit Bloomgarden produced the comedy at the Shubert Theater, New York City.

THE GRISETTE (Odette Joyeux), or *süßes Mädel*, and THE POET (Jean-Louis Barrault) have their turn together in the famous 1950 film "La Ronde," based on *Hands Around*. Max Ophuls was the director.

OPPOSITE: THEODOR (Peter Weck), CHRISTINE (Christiane Hörbiger), and MIZZI (Hannelore Fischer) in the 1966 production of *Light-O'-Love* at the Schauspielhaus in Zurich. The production was directed by Wolfgang Glück.

GENIA (Heidemarie Hatheyer) confronts her hus-
band, HOFREITER (Adolf Wohlbrück), in *The
Vast Domain*. This 1964 production at the Thalia-
Theater in Hamburg was directed by Gustav Manker.
ROSEMARIE CLAUSEN

OPPOSITE: MIZZI (Vilma Degischer) and LOLO
LANGHUBER (Helly Servi) in a scene from the
one-acter *Countess Mizzi, or The Family Reunion*.
Heinrich Schnitzler directed this 1964 production at
the Theater in der Josefstadt in Vienna.
BARBARA PFLAUM

BERNHARDI (Ernst Deutsch) and REDER (Kurt
Buecheler), the priest, in a 1955 production of *Professor Bernhardi*. Directed by Heinrich Schnitzler at
the Theater am Kurfürstendamm, Berlin.
FOTO JLSE BUHS

# THE ONE-ACT PLAYS

One-act plays combined into a cycle is a form that lies deep within my nature (and I do not mean this at all jestingly). Just look at my plays from this point of view: Many of my single-acters are remarkably well-rounded to a degree never achieved by any of my longer plays. Instead of firmly joined links of a chain, my single-acters represent more or less precious stones that are strung together—not interlocked by necessity but sequentially arranged as neighbors on the same ribbon.

Thus wrote Arthur Schnitzler on 1 October 1905 to Otto Brahm. The contrast between links of a chain and precious stones on a ribbon refers to the difference between the earlier cycles (*Anatol* and *Hands Around*), in which the characters formed the unifying connection, and the later "cycles," which were collections of the one-act plays written between 1894 and 1904. In these

works the themes rather than the characters con-
nect the plays. They remain, however, independent
works that can be performed individually or in different combinations. They are variations on a given
theme, answers to the question of the genuineness
of human behavior, whether it be in the form of
artistic creativity, one's relationship to one's fellow-
man, or submission to a predetermined fate.

The one-act form enabled Schnitzler to depict
the lightninglike emergence of a situation, to keep
the plot within narrow limits, and to isolate a problem. This form is more appropriate to an inner
rather than to an external concern. Schnitzler's
choice of form has no connection with his alleged
inability to sustain the action in a longer work, a
shortcoming for which he has often been re-
proached, but rather stems from his desire to il-
luminate a theme from many sides.

*The Eccentric*
(Die überspannte Person)

In *The Eccentric* (written, 1894) the two
characters, He and She, are having an affair with
one another. They meet in a furnished room. She is

married but on this occasion has to confess to him that she is expecting his child. For him, who neither can nor wants to assume responsibility for the child, this is no problem, since after all she is married and will have a father for her child. He has not considered, however, that she took their affair seriously and has been refusing herself to her husband. He advises her to make up for this neglect and accuses her of being "eccentric" when she punishes him for his advice with a show of contempt. He knows better: "She will follow my advice nevertheless! . . ."

He demands that she substitute a lie in place of their asserting their parenthood. Just as Anatol did in *Dying Pangs*, she loses her illusion of eternal love. Like Gabriele in *The Lonely Way* she is abandoned before the birth of her child. She is "eccentric" because she does not prefer convenience to love.

## Half Past One
(Halbzwei)

*Half Past One* (written, 1894) is a *Taglied* (song of lovers parting at daybreak) with shifted accents. It is still night, and he does not complain because he must leave, for he is accustomed to that—even the *Taglied* loses its plaintiveness if it is repeated. He no longer regards being with his mistress as the *summum bonum*, and "a smile of happiness passes over his face" when he finds the street entrance to his apartment house still unlocked so that he can get into his own bed more quickly.

This is the dialogue of two people who loved each other yesterday but for whom today's convenience means more than yesterday's passion. The dialogue consists of their attempt to conceal this from each other. It is the continuation of a dialogue in *Hands Around*. The partners have not separated. The hollow expressions of love have become stale. They accuse each other of indifference. *Hands Around* means love for one night. *Half Past One* means the same love every night. He must pay for the highest moment with an arduous nightly journey home and weariness the next day. But it is precisely the homeward journey that is the proof of his bachelorhood, the symbol of his freedom.

## Paracelsus

The theme of this one-act play, written in 1897, was already treated in the first scene of the *Anatol* cycle. Through the magic of Paracelsus, the smith Cyprian becomes aware of uncertainties that threaten man through his dreams and wishes. Cyprian is not as sure of his wife as he thought. Cyprian says: "It was a game, and yet I found its meaning."

Paracelsus, by virtue of his magical power, is one of those puppeteers who play with human souls. He stands above chance and cannot lose any illusions because he has none. He stands above the game. "I can be fate whenever it pleases me!"

There is scarcely a book about Schnitzler that does not include the final speech of Paracelsus, which all critics have interpreted as Schnitzler's personal attitude:

What's not a game that here below we're
 playing,

> Profound and great as it may seem to be!
> The one does play with hosts of violent
> soldiers;
> Another plays with superstitious fools;
> And yet another plays with suns and stars—
> I play with human souls. Yet he alone
> Will meaning find who seeks the meaning
> in it.
> There flow together dream and waking
> time,
> Truth and deception. Certainty is nowhere.
> Nothing we know of others, of ourselves no
> more;
> We always play—and wise is he who
> knows.

Schnitzler was not wrong when he complained: "One takes out of context any single speech by a character and acts as if this one speech contained the author's viewpoint or even expressed his *Weltanschauung*. For example: 'We always play—and wise is he who knows' is said by Paracelsus, but not by me."

And Paracelsus teaches this lesson superciliously, brimming with pride, which makes him feel superior to generals, clergymen, and God, whom he doubts. Many of Schnitzler's characters have accepted this theory of life as one of play-acting. This is not a profession of Schnitzler's creed but rather the hypothesis of the characters. That everyone is acting is the credo of those characters who engage in play-acting. And it is this credo that causes the ruination of the many characters in Schnitzler's works who do not play-act.

## His Helpmate
### (Die Gefährtin)

*His Helpmate* (written, 1898) takes place on the evening following the burial of Professor Pilgram's wife. Pilgram discovers, not that his wife had an affair with his assistant—that was something he had known and approved of because of her youth—but that his assistant had for some time been secretly engaged to another woman. He knew that his wife was not able to be simply a man's helpmate, and thus he had allowed her to give her love to a younger man. Only when he realizes that the assistant did not take the affair seriously does he fire him in the belief that his wife had known nothing about the other woman. He learns, however, that she both knew and accepted the double game of the assistant. Pilgram had overcome his conventional views of marriage and fidelity and, because he believed her to be happy, had concealed his wife's affair behind the cloak of marriage. Now he is forced to acknowledge that she had voluntarily entered into a game that did not entail emotional involvement and that served only as a mechanical satisfaction of instinctive drives. Although she has been dead for only a short time, the physical appearance of his helpmate has already receded for Pilgram into the distance. He had known nothing about the woman who was closest to him.

## New Year's Eve
### (Sylvesternacht)

In *New Year's Eve* (written, 1900) the young son of the house, Emil, has arranged with his girl friend that they would both look at a certain star on New Year's Eve because they could not be together. Agathe, whose husband is the cousin of Emil's mother, comes upon Emil while he is engaged in this romantic rendezvous and brings him back to reality:

AGATHE: Why are you not with her?
EMIL: Madame, that is simply impossible because of the way circumstances are.

AGATHE: And I tell you, you do not love your absent sweetheart, otherwise it would not be impossible.

By way of example she tells him about a woman who on New Year's Eve went for a drive in the Prater with her lover, although she had a house full of guests. She had let matters reach the point where she risked her marriage and wealth for her love.

Emil lives in his illusion of the future, Agathe in her memories. False sentimentality on his part, confession on hers. At the same time he learns how life is and how it should be. During the conversation they draw closer to one another. Future and past meet in the moment, "their lips touch as if by chance." He has been urged to action, and this emboldens him. Thereupon his "deed" is turned back into illusion.

Agathe asks: "Do you perhaps flatter yourself that *you* were the one I kissed?" The kiss was imagination. There is no difference between the meeting in the stars and this kiss. There was no reality in either.

## *Living Hours*
(Lebendige Stunden)

The *Living Hours* (*Lebendige Stunden*) cycle originated in the years 1900 and 1901. It is comprised of four plays: a conversational play (*Living Hours*); a play involving a flashback (*The Lady with the Dagger*); a play built around a rehearsal (*Last Masks*); and a farce (*Literature*). These works are variations on the attitude of men toward death and toward life. In *Living Hours* death precedes the play. In *The Lady with the Dagger* death will occur after the play, when the vision is fulfilled. *Last Masks* presents death on the stage with the dying man relinquishing his remaining vanity and malicious joy in the sufferings of others. *Literature* concerns two hack writers who play with love; themes from the previous three acts—writing based on personal experience, jealousy, and vanity—are taken up again and parodied.

.    .

In *Living Hours* a mother has committed suicide for her son, Heinrich. She has ended her suffering in order to keep him from grieving over her suffering. For her son is a poet who possibly because of her cannot find the strength to write. Her friend Hausdorfer betrays the cause of her death to Heinrich, although it had been the mother's will never to let Heinrich learn anything about it. But Hausdorfer has lost his friend to death, and his hatred for Heinrich, for whose sake she died, is greater than his respect for the dead woman's wishes. He is the injured party—she did not remain alive for his sake but died for her son's. This attitude places the figure of Hausdorfer in an ambiguous light. The magnanimity of the mother is tarnished by the arrogance of the son, who takes her sacrifice for granted. Whether his work justified a death seems doubtful.

The concluding speeches, however, transcend the psychological weaknesses of the two conversational partners; two opinions confront each other and each adduces well-reasoned arguments. Who will permit himself to judge which view is correct?

> HAUSDORFER: What is all your scribbling, and even if you are the greatest genius, what is that compared to an hour, a living hour, in which your mother sat here in her armchair and spoke to us or, for that matter, was silent—but she was here! And she lived, lived!
>
> HEINRICH: Living hours? They do not live longer

than the last person who remembers them. It is
not the worst profession to make such hours
endure beyond their time. . . .

## *The Lady with the Dagger*
(Die Frau mit dem Dolche)

This work also involves the transformation
of an experience into a work of art. Pauline sees
the meaning of her life in existing for her husband,
who is a writer. Because she believes in him, she
accepts the sacrifice that she must be available for
him only at those times when he needs her as a
wife—or as subject matter. They have vowed as
marriage partners to confess every impulse of their
soul to each other. He makes a new play out of her
confessions and thus would be even more grateful
to her for lapses, because he could exploit them:
"He would be the man to unite both." She defends
him to Leonhard, who would like to become her
lover. For the artist everything serves as material,
the whole world enters into his work through the
filter of his artistic soul. He absorbs life from the

people around him and transposes it into art. This thought is brought home to them both in a profound manner through the contemplation of art. Standing before a Renaissance painting while waiting to meet Leonhard, Pauline has a vision of an artist who is a titan and who transforms life into art. In her vision, she becomes Paola, the lady with the dagger in the painting. Paola is the wife of the artist, Remigio, and she knows that when the picture for which she is sitting as model is completed, "then I will be nothing, will be used up, while my living being pulsates in that picture." But the artist utilizes not only life but also death—that is, the death of others. Thus, through the death of Lionardo, whom Paola kills with her dagger while Remigio looks on, Remigio receives the inspiration that finally makes it possible for him to complete his painting.

## Last Masks
(Die letzten Masken)

Rademacher, a journalist who has fallen on hard times, lies on his deathbed. He has summoned his former friend and competitor Weihgast, a successful writer, to the hospital in order to tell him the truth: the wife of this famous author had deceived him with Rademacher. While Rademacher may have failed as an artist, in life he stole the celebrity's wife without his noticing it.

Before Weihgast arrives, Rademacher rehearses his performance, he practices his quickness at repartee, his rhetoric, and rehearses the technique of unmasking his victim. His sick roommate, an actor who is intrigued by the idea of such a rehearsal, gives him his cues.

Rademacher does not get beyond the rehearsal. He makes no use of the occasion of the visit of his friend, who spreads out before him his vanity, his ambition, and his sensibility. Rademacher realizes how useless revenge would be: "What do people like us have to do with people who will still be alive tomorrow?" He no longer plays the game. It would have been his last masquerade if he had told Weihgast the truth. He would have been using the truth to serve his joy at the sufferings of others and his lust for revenge. In the face of death, he has seen through the emptiness of the game of life.

## *Literature*
(Literatur)

*Literature* is without doubt the merriest of Schnitzler's plays, and yet it has one of his most important concerns for its theme: the responsibility of the poet and the perversion of truthfulness by hack writers. In his typology *The Mind in Words and Actions* he juxtaposes the negative type, the hack writer, with the positive type, represented by the poet. Between the two groups lies an uncrossable dividing line, so that hack writers can never reach the status of poets, even though there are seeming exceptions. A hack writer can, "under the influence of a strong personal experience, produce a genuine poetic effect in one or another of his works. Never, however, will such a deception last for long, and the expert often sees through it at the very moment it is attempted and is succeeding with the popular audience." Experience here means a special, striking, extraordinary —even if not unusual—formative impression, a change in the environment that affects people and is perceived as fate.

In *Literature* two such hack writers are placed on the stage in an exaggerated situation, to be heartily ridiculed. The public can laugh all the more easily, since the subject is not one of close concern: hack writers who evaluate their love experiences in advance with respect to their eventual usability as literature. They do everything twice. They both experience and formulate their experience—simultaneously, insofar as possible. That is to say, while they are embracing, they are already coining phrases in their mind. At the same time, they naturally preserve the illusion of unalloyed feeling—the partner is not supposed to notice anything. They write their letters to each other in the evening, before their eyes fall shut. Then, after they ostensibly can no longer keep their eyes open, they make a copy of their letter. This is published in their next novel, which appears after the passage of the required length of time needed to write enough letters to fill a medium-sized novel.

The play opens with a dialogue between Margarete, a hack writer from Schwabing, and Klemens, a Viennese aristocrat whom she is about to marry. Klemens's greatest pride is that he does not read books. He had picked Margarete up in Munich and has stipulated as a condition of their impending marriage that she never write again. She considers herself an artist, for after all she has published a small volume of love poems. But the sight of these poems arouses in Klemens a natural feeling of embarrassment. He does not want to have the love experiences of his bride on his fireplace mantle—even though in his naiveté he considers them to be fictitious. In the course of their dialogue Margarete reveals that she could not suppress her desire to write and has produced a novel that, moreover, has already been published. Klemens wants to have the entire printing destroyed.

The hack writer Gilbert visits Margarete, who once had been his mistress. He has also written a novel—the purpose was the novel, the mistress the means. Gilbert, however, did not reckon with the possibility that she likewise was using him with the same purpose in mind. Since the two have used the same letters, two identical novels now exist. Margarete's engagement is endangered once again, but she is able to escape this threat: as proof of her love for Klemens, she burns the one remaining copy of her novel, which Klemens did not have destroyed with the rest. The incorrigible Gilbert regrets not having found such a clever conclusion for his "work."

*The Puppeteer*
(Der Puppenspieler)

Under the title *Marionettes* (*Marionetten*) Schnitzler collected three one-act plays that were written during the years from 1902 to 1904: *The Puppeteer*, a play about toying with human souls; *Gallant Cassian*, a puppet play; and *The Big Wurstel Puppet Theater*, a play within a play (a puppet play on Schnitzlerian themes, with audience).

.  .

*The Puppeteer* was originally intended for inclusion in the *Living Hours* cycle. Here, too, as in the one-acter *Living Hours*, the main figure is a poet, but one whose precious writing is in real life and not on paper. He manipulates people, unites them into couples whose children he considers his creations. He is not content to restrict the game to his own imagination. He plays with living examples of the scenes created in his fantasy. He himself is not bound to life but stands above it in the consciousness of his creative power.

Eleven years ago, the "puppeteer" Georg Merklin had introduced his shy friend to a girl:

> "You were puppets in my hand. I pulled the strings. It was arranged that she would pretend to fall in love with you, for I had always felt sorry for you Eduard. I wanted to awaken within you the illusion of happiness, so that true happiness, when it finally appeared, would find you ready. And thus—as a result of the talent that may be given to people like me—I possibly produced a greater effect than I intended. I made you into another person. And let me say: it is a nobler pleasure to play with living creatures than to cause imaginative figures to whirl about in poetic dance."

It turns out that the girl married Merklin's friend. The game became reality, and now the puppeteer must face the destruction of *his* illusion. He does not have people like puppets on strings after all. Embittered, he retreats into his life of chance and uncertainty but of inner freedom.

## Gallant Cassian
(Der tapfere Cassian)

The puppet play allows the possibility of exaggerating and of laying it on thick. Puppets do not act according to the laws of probability, there are no motivations for their actions, they are directed by whoever controls their wires. Thus, the puppet play becomes a symbol of life with its adventures and chance occurrences.

Martin, a student and lucky gambler, plans to desert his girl, Sophie, in order to win a notorious dancer. His cousin, the soldier Cassian, who has escaped many dangers, visits Martin before his departure. Sophie, who has heard wonderful things about Cassian, throws herself into his arms. Cassian wins everything from the student and stabs him in addition. In the figure of Sophie, luck has jumped from Martin, who lives as an introvert, to Cassian, who acts as an extrovert. But in the morning Cassian, too, will desert Sophie for the dancer.

## The Big Wurstel Puppet Theater
(Zum großen Wurstel)

In the Prater a new puppet theater has been established. The actors who play the puppets hang by wires. A puppet play that trivializes Schnitzler's themes is being performed. In it the hero is facing a duel with the Duke, who wrongly accuses him of a love affair with the Duchess. Actually, the Duke is having an affair with the *süßes Mädel*, whom the hero loves. On the night before the duel, the Duchess visits the hero because she wants to experience the love for which he is to die. But the Duke has recognized his error and withdraws from the duel, whereupon the Duchess is no longer attracted to the hero. The hero, however, now wants to die, since the *süßes Mädel* also deserts him. The puppets recite motifs from *The Veil of Beatrice* and *The Call of Life* in the clumsy verses of a poet who sits in the audience in front of the puppet stage. He acts like one of the spectators, who accompany the play with their well-meaning, acrimonious, or naive commentaries and who at the same time remain aware that they, too, are only types. All are invented and directed by the poet and yet act as if they were alive. The play concludes, however, by showing that neither the puppets who rebel against the poet controlling them, nor the poet, nor the audience are independently alive. All are now puppets in the hands of a higher power. Everyone falls victim to the "Unknown Visitor," who comes at the end and cuts through the visible and invisible wires.

> This sword, however, makes it clear
> Who was a puppet, who was human here.
> This cut severs even invisible wire,
> To many a proud puppeteer's ire!

Everything that is said is retracted, canceled out. What remains is the feeling of a threatening emptiness. Nothing is certain. People are puppets in the hands of fate, whose representative is horrified by his own mysterious power.

## Countess Mizzi, or The Family Reunion
(Komtesse Mizzi, oder Der Familientag)

This ironical "Comedy in One Act," written in 1907, draws a conclusion from the theory of society as being a game—the society that lives according to aesthetic principles and is organized according to moral conventions. The immoral games —the liaison and the affair—are eventually subverted by morality and even become established as unions based on ethical principles. If the unions were of this nature from the beginning, the interaction of the now middle-aged love pairs, who, as the curtain goes up on the play, either separate (as do the count and his mistress of many years) or find each other again, would really be a family reunion. But there still are no traditional unions. Mizzi, the daughter of the count, will perhaps marry the man who is the father of her child. The child meets his mother for the first time only after he has grown up and has graduated from high school. Schnitzler "suppresses the recognition scene between the unwed mother and her grown son, a scene for whose sake alone most other dramatists would have carried out such an idea at all" (Siegfried Jacobsen).

Countess Mizzi lived through a difficult time when her newborn child was taken from her and the prince was not ready to marry her. But all of this happened a long time ago. Now that the prince wants to marry her, she is not interested. She has overcome her tribulations and has adapted to this society, which disregards feelings for the sake of social conventions and then circumvents the conventions by opting for noncommittal relationships. The aristocratic bearing of the countess prevents her from suffering a fate such as Christine's in *Light-O'-Love* or from behaving like an "eccentric."

*The Hour of Recognition*
(Stunde des Erkennens)

In 1915 Schnitzler combined the three one-act plays *The Hour of Recognition, The Big*

*Scene,* and *The Festival of Bacchus* under the title *Comedies of Words* (*Komödie der Worte*). Schnitzler had always observed the way words were used and abused and brought this theme to expression in his works. Words, which represent both a means of communication and at the same time the medium of drama as conversation plays in Schnitzler's sense, are shown in their dubiousness and murderous effect not only in these plays, but also in *The Word* (*Das Wort*), an uncompleted drama based on the life of Peter Altenberg. In this work the protagonist, the coffeehouse poet Treuenhof, drives the young painter Willi to suicide by his irresponsible chatter. The first play in *Comedies of Words* involves a similar situation—that is, the destruction of a human life; the second concerns the falsification of truth by the art of acting, which knows how to make lies sound genuine; the third deals with the rescue of a marriage through the medium of the word. In all three one-act plays someone deceives others with the help of words.

Concerning the *Comedies of Words* the great Austrian actor Josef Kainz wrote in 1937:

> The fundamental, unifying idea is the recognition that human beings are constantly acting out comedies with one another. They cannot escape acting, and most people do not themselves know where truth ceases and deception begins. For this masquerade words offer the best means of concealment; they lie, shimmer in a thousand colors,

falsify the circumstances of reality, and make deception easy. From the beginning of his career as a writer, Schnitzler made it his task both to unmask the various kinds of word comedies that people are accustomed to perform before one another and to demonstrate with ironic skepticism the falseness of big words and conventional phrases. The themes of lying and unmasking belong to the main concerns of his writings.

· ·

In *Hour of Recognition* Dr. Eckold, who had kept silent about the fact that he believes his wife, Klara, to be guilty of adultery with his colleague Ormin, finally confronts her. Now that their daughter is married he sees no further reason to continue to live with his wife. She actually has not deceived him although she did love Ormin. During the last ten years her husband had not considered her as a wife but had maintained their relationship only for the sake of his daughter.

> KLARA: You had the right—perhaps—to drive me away, maybe even to kill me. But the right to keep silent about the punishment that you deigned to inflict upon me—that right you did not have. You have deceived me worse and a thousand times more cowardly than I you. You have degraded me more deeply than a human being may degrade another person!

Eckold followed the path of convenience. Instead of confronting Ormin, whose entire life he feels as "an insult to himself," he chooses the easy form of revenge and repudiates his wife. Klara leaves without a word of farewell: "To no one. Words lie."

*The Big Scene*
(Große Szene)

While everyone in society is compelled to play a role, the actor has the right and the ability to change roles—that is his profession. Just as he plays one role after the other in the theater, so does he also have the possibility of doing the same thing in life, and he uses this capability to his own advantage. For the distinction between acting on the stage and deception in life is too fine for anyone to detect at first glance. The actor refuses to accept any responsibility for his deception while acting in life, since—either out of self-deception or calculation—he regards acting in life the same as acting on the stage. Yet, there is a difference between the world of acting—out of which one can step at any moment, so that sooner or later the acting is recognizable as such—and the world of deception, of hypocrisy, out of which one cannot step without endangering one's life, without risking the security of one's existence. Acting on the stage is cheerful, a masquerade, a fancy dress ball, transparent and noncommittal. Deception is final, the role can no longer be separated from the person, one falls captive to it, is caught up in it, so that if one gives up the role, he gives up himself.

When the performer removes his mask, everything is revealed to have been only a play (". . . a Viennese masquerade and nothing more"). For the actor, however, these two realms are interchangeable. He does not see the separation, he does not hold to the distinction; he regards deception and acting as the same thing. What he does every evening on the stage, he also does every day in life: he performs. He is surprised when his "performances" are considered deceptions and sovereignly extricates himself from an affair by means of his acting genius.

While on vacation the famous actor Herbot deceived his wife with a young girl, whose fiancé now wants to call him to account. Herbot and the girl protected themselves in advance, however, by means of a forged letter. Moreover, Herbot plays the innocent so convincingly that the fiancé departs satisfied. Although his wife, Sophie, is reduced to despair, she nevertheless remains with

Herbot, for he cannot live without her, as he assures her with a profusion of words.

## The Festival of Bacchus
(Das Bacchusfest)

The poet Felix Staufner has withdrawn into isolation for several weeks in order to complete a work. Spending this time at a vacation resort, his wife, Agnes, has met and fallen in love with Guido, a wealthy man. The plot situation of *Literature* is repeated: the woman caught between the poet and the sportsman, between insecurity and a well-established home life, between loneliness and the security of bourgeois society. In this play, however, Agnes decides in favor of a life of anxiety at the side of the poet instead of following her honorable attraction to the other man.

The motivation for Agnes's return to Felix is anticipated early in the play. She tells Guido: "That is just the way he is. When a work seriously preoccupies him, then everything else fades into oblivion." Though Agnes suffers when Felix is away for weeks at a time, she has learned to prefer it: "It made me feel much more uncomfortable when he remained at home and still left me alone. When I became, as it were, a shadow in his eyes . . . more pale, more lifeless, than any character that he had just invented. When, as it were, I felt as if I were ceasing to exist . . . in his eyes . . ." The term "in his eyes" is decisive for her return to her husband.

Meanwhile, the flirtation that Guido and Agnes have engaged in while on their vacation, has been given timeless form in a mythological drama by Felix, who is not unaware of his wife's affair. The new play, "The Festival of Bacchus," concerns the sacred grove where pagan men and women meet for one night each year. On the next morning each must return again to his customary life and forget the partner of the night before, or, if he should decide for the new partner, he must never again try to return to his previous life.

Felix wins Agnes back by narrating the plot of his play to her. In *The Lady with the Dagger*, life in the form of a murder had made possible the completion of a work of art. But here the situation has been reversed: through his art, Felix has had an effect on life.

## The Green Cockatoo
(Der grüne Kakadu)

No play has ever so thoroughly blended history and theater, complete deception and transparent playacting, threadbare politics and uninhibited pleasure as *The Green Cockatoo*, Schnitzler's one-act play written in 1898, concerning the outbreak of the French Revolution. The richness of content makes it appear as if five acts have been compressed into one. Frivolity and despair, prostitution and gambling with death, real deception and stage-acting, illusion and truthfulness are all brought masterfully together.

The virtuosity of the scene construction and the differentiation of the characters have found perfect expression here in a few pages. Every character has his own unmistakable face, his unique manner of expression. None of the characters is interchangeable, none is a one-dimensional figure, each one is a rounded individual. Each character leads his own life, none is decoration, a mere bringer of cues. Yet all are dependent upon one another and are so interrelated that a missing dialogue would tear a perceptible hole into the fabric created out of plot and configuration.

*The Green Cockatoo* breathes the air of a transitional period, of the turning to a new century, and combines the sensitivity of an aristocratic society with coarse theatrical representations. The time of the play is 14 July 1789. In a cellar tavern, The Green Cockatoo, which is frequented by members of the aristocracy, a play is being performed for the guests. Revolt is presented as titillation, but what is actually meant is revolution. Here performers act out crimes that are already being committed on the street, still unknown to the noble guests. Down below in the tavern the action takes place and the cards are being put on the table. Falsehood and deceit (in the figure of the threadbare politician) are not needed here; we are in a world of stage-acting. *The Green Cockatoo* is a reflection of appearance and reality. The actors mingle with the guests and talk with them, but each remains always within his role. The public is not impersonal. The actors are only partly playing roles: the girls are not entirely acting but are actually consorting with the nobles.

The owner of the tavern, a former theater director, is actor and stage director at the same time in this tavern performance. He arranges the scenes during the extemporaneous performance of his actors. His relationship to his public is not that of an artist but rather that of a socio-political critic. Although he pretends that his speeches of denunciation against the aristocrats are acting, they are actually intended seriously. On the other hand, Grasset, a former member of the tavern-owner's troupe who has stopped in the tavern for a drink, conceals his acting ability by passing it off as truthfulness in his new profession as a public orator. If the revolution should fail, bringing his role to an end, Grasset intends to become a professional actor again. Even now he has remained basically an actor. He lives from applause. Of the two, the tavern-owner is the actual revolutionary. But he only acts out the revolution on the stage; he tells the truth without acting upon it in reality.

The tavern-owner's actors play the parts of the revolutionaries, who outside the doors of the tavern are actually about to storm the Bastille. The performance is not intended to upset but to titillate the audience of nobles, who applaud the play about their own destruction. The tavern-owner does not produce political theater exclusively—or the police would have to interfere. He spices it with erotic stimulants (all of the actresses represent prostitutes, which they also are in reality, with the exception of Georgette) and criminal scenes that are supposed to arouse the jaded senses of the blasé nobles. This is his concession to the paying public that he despises.

The spectators share the stage with the actors

and therefore can feel the illusion of reality more strongly than in a regular theater. But at the same time they can remain conscious of the fact that they do not have to take the play seriously. The members of the audience are not personally involved. The danger that they might become involved in the action stimulates them, but they are reassured by remembering that it is only a play and therefore know they will not become involved. Or rather, they shudder at the thought that they might be drawn into the action anyway, and thus they enjoy the mixed emotions of fear and security. These two possibilities for the public to react to the play—calmness at the consciousness that play and reality are strictly separated and enjoyment of the disturbing suspicion that appearance and reality are blended—are realized in François and in the poet Rollin.

François knows how to distinguish play from reality. He is both guide and companion to Albin, who cannot distinguish between the two realms. Rollin overcomes his recognition of the distinction in order to enjoy the interpenetration of the two spheres. Rollin's companion, the Marquise, matches Albin in naiveté: she enjoys simply, he thinks simple-mindedly; she lives truthfully, he seeks the truth. Rollin does not enter into the play; François plays along and accepts the premises of the *joke* of the tavern-owner; Albin is horrified and confused. The Marquis is conscious of the sphere of the play but does not enjoy it because the performance embarrasses him. The Marquise would love to participate, but for her this would not be acting because she does not need to dissemble. If she were to remain only a spectator, then she would be pretending, behaving contrary to her true nature.

For the Duke, who arrives later, play and reality resemble each other: "Everything is only true at the very moment that it happens." Thus, in his view the comedian, who can be a different person at every instant, is "more than all of us." Grain, a murderer just out of prison, cannot act. Gaston, the actor from whom Grain had heard of the troupe while still in prison, cannot steal. Although Gaston had acted the part of a pickpocket every evening, he was caught when he tried an actual theft for the first time. Both are dilettantes. The one has been able to assume the role of a thief and make it evident to his audience that he was a thief; the other has the capability of stealing in reality, a technique that might be destroyed were he capable of making it evident, as an actor must do. One cannot see in a capable thief that he is a thief. The actor only appears as a thief when he represents one.

Everyone plays the part of something that he is not. They play roles and in the process are good or honest or dissolute. Henri, the star of the troupe, has assumed a role that is tailor-made for his ability. In reality he wants to give up acting because he has married Leocadie. But she deceives him with the Duke while he is giving this, his farewell performance. Henri is acting the part of a deceived husband, which he actually is but does not know that he is. He falls victim to self-deception. He does not playact in life. He wants to be true, genuine, and faithful. He does not identify with his part when he performs. Not for a moment has he lost his awareness that he is playing a role, and not for a moment has he forgotten life. He does not disguise the rolelike quality of his performance, he declaims in a theatrical manner. He believes that their marriage has produced a transformation in Leocadie, whose past life he knows. This is where his error begins. He will not admit to himself that Leocadie could deceive him, but he acts it out nevertheless—that is to say, he only imagines the deception.

The others do not notice that Henri is acting because they know that the deception is true. He tells of his private revolt against the desecration of marriage by the aristocracy and of murdering the Duke, and all believe he is really telling the truth. Even the tavern-owner believes the murder to be real and urges Henri in all sincerity, though still in character with his role, to flee. François, too, knows of the deception, but he alone is able to recognize the murder as only part of the play. Therefore, he must hail the tavern-owner's warning as a successful part of the play. At last Henri is made aware that his act is the truth, and now he actually does kill the Duke when the latter finally arrives at the tavern. Henri thus becomes the hero of the revolution.

. .

From the beginning an effort was made to separate Schnitzler's one-act plays from their cycles—they were performed singly, put together in different combinations (as happened with *Literature* and *The Big Scene*), or performed with short works of other dramatists. One reason for this might have been because *The Green Cockatoo*, after its premiere with *Paracelsus* and *His Help-mate* on 1 March 1899 at Vienna's Burgtheater, was not released to other Vienna theaters (*The Green Cockatoo* was also published with *Paracelsus* and *His Helpmate* in 1899). Or perhaps the reason was simply that the one-act plays were so successful individually.

At the Burgtheater, apart from the three one-acters collected under the over-all title *The Green Cockatoo*, only *Comedies of Words* was presented as a cycle. This premiere took place on 12 October 1915.

*The Puppeteer*, which had been premiered at the Deutsches Theater in Berlin in 1903, received its first performance at the Burgtheater on 8 May 1929 (together with *Faun* by Hermann Bahr and *Schöne Seelen* by Felix Salten) under the direction of Hans Brahm, a nephew of Otto Brahm.

From the cycle *Living Hours* (the entire cycle

had been given its premiere in 1902 at Berlin's Deutsches Theater), *Literature* was first performed at the Burgtheater on 31 January 1914 under the direction of Albert Heine (together with Franz Wedekind's *Kammersänger* and Georges Courteline's *Boubourouche*). And on 15 November 1931, at a presentation in memory of Arthur Schnitzler, *Last Masks* from the same cycle was performed under Heine's direction.

To the present time *Countess Mizzi* (premiered at Vienna's Deutsches Volkstheater in 1909) has been performed twice in the Burgtheater: for the first time on 23 March 1927 together with Ferenc Molnar's *Veilchen;* then together with *Light-O'-Love* on 12 June 1954. Regarding the combination with *Light-O'-Love*, O. M. Fontana wrote in *Presse* on 15 June 1954: "Just like the musician's daughter, Christine, Countess Mizzi in her youth experiences the destruction of a complete love by a half love. She was not destroyed by this but only became a female eccentric, participating now in the half love, because it is part of life, but despising it."

On 2 February 1930 there was an evening of Schnitzler's one-act plays in the Burgtheater: *Paracelsus, The Green Cockatoo, The Big Scene*. Even in 1930 one did not yet dare to perform *The Green Cockatoo* in unabridged form (in 1898 it had been banned by the censor in Berlin). On this issue Raoul Auernheimer, with reference to the quiet scandal at the premiere in 1899, wrote in the *Neue Freie Presse* on 4 February 1930: "A fabulously clever Duke and a lustful Marquise aroused equally vigorous objection from both ends of the spectrum. Now the matter has been solved in a different manner by letting them appear, to be sure, though softened."

Five one-act plays, three of them from Schnitzler's literary estate, were directed by Heinrich Schnitzler on 29 March 1932 at the Deutsches Volkstheater in Vienna: *The Murderess, Those Who Glide, The Eccentric, Half Past One,* and *Anatol's Megalomania.* After his return from the United States he produced on 9 March 1960 in the Theater in der Josefstadt the combination of the one-acters *The Green Cockatoo* and *Literature,* and on 26 October 1960 the cycle *Comedies of Words* was performed in the same theater.

In a one-act evening "Days of Memory" on 31 August 1962, Heinrich Schnitzler directed *Last Masks* together with Anton Wildgans's *In Ewigkeit Amen* and Johann Nestroy's *Frühere Verhältnisse.*

Among Schnitzler's one-acters, *Literature* and *The Green Cockatoo* have been of most interest to American producers. *Literature's* first English-language performance in New York was in 1908, under the title *The Literary Sense.* In 1914 it was produced at the Little Theater in Philadelphia. The Washington Square Players revived the short play in 1915, presenting it on a bill of four one-act comedies at the Bandbox Theater in New York. One critic summed up both the play and the production by noting that *Literature* was a comedy "smartly written and full of Bohemian atmosphere that even the amateur interpretation it received could not destroy." *Literature* was not seen again on the American stage until 1931, this time in a presentation by the Cornell Dramatic Club in Ithaca, New York.

*The Green Cockatoo* was more popular with American theater directors and gained more attention from the critics than *Literature*. It was first offered to American audiences in an English-language production in New York in 1910. The then-popular Minnie Maddern Fiske and the Manhattan Company staged the one-acter at the Lyceum Theater on a double bill with Gerhart Hauptmann's *Hannele*. Although most of the critics' remarks were directed at the inadequate acting or at the "stilted and unnatural" translation, the play was spoken of as "an agreeable surprise. . . ." Walter P. Eaton called Schnitzler, on the basis of this play, "a man with a keen theatric sense, a neat, nervous, direct style, and a gift of ironic humor."

*The Green Cockatoo* was again produced in 1917 at the Pabst Theater in Milwaukee—a production that also included *The Lady with a Dagger* and *The Farewell Supper* from the *Anatol* cycle. In 1924 it was offered at Le Petit Théâtre in New Orleans.

In 1930 *The Green Cockatoo* was utilized as a curtain raiser when the Civic Repertory Theater billed it with *Lady from Alfaqueque*, by the Álvarez Quintero brothers. Perhaps because the Álvarez Quintero comedy had already been established as a successful feature of the company's repertory, it was Schnitzler's "well-known one-act playlet" that drew the critical attention of the reviewers. The play was staged by the famous Eva Le Gallienne, at that time director of the company, and the costumes and scenery were designed by Aline Bernstein (now probably best known to the public for her relationship with Thomas Wolfe). Egon Brecher was cast as the tavern-owner, Burgess Meredith as Grain, and Jacob Ben-Ami as Henri. The critic for the *New York Herald Tribune*, who thought the performance "colorful, tense and exceedingly well acted" and the direction of the entire cast quite skillful, stood alone in his opinion. John Mason Brown, of the *New York Evening Post*, considered Miss Le Gallienne's selection of *The Green Cockatoo* unwise. He accused the actors and the director of making too little effort to interpret Schnitzler:

> . . . this short drama of Schnitzler's is as exacting in the demands that it makes of the acting forces of an organization as it is relentless in its calls for virtuoso direction. Indeed, the richness and the implication of the play are limited only by the implication and the richness that are brought to it in performance.
>
> Schnitzler spins his tale ironically, sends it laughing through the shadows of its make-believe until

the flames signalizing the rabble's triumph at the Bastille stream through the windows of the wine cellar and cast their red light on the grim tragedy that has taken place within. He tells it, too, in terms of many characters that are sketches for actors to work from rather than finished portraits, and with a deep reliance upon a director's ordering of its crowds and reading of its subtleties. . . . neither Miss Le Gallienne as a director or her acting company does more than sketch in the barest outlines of the play which Schnitzler has written. . . . down on Fourteenth Street "The Green Cockatoo" never ceases to be anything but a very vehement high school pageant of the French Revolution; a kind of one-finger exercise in producing à la Reinhardt, played with the little finger at that.

The critic for the *World* accused the company of having widely missed the mark in their interpretation of Schnitzler's intentions:

It is difficult to believe that in this sketch the author's intentions were anything but slyly humorous—it seems to emerge as a derisive study of melodramatic passions played above an accompaniment of mutterings from the reign of terror. The group last night, however, acted it with all the sound and fury of a desperate tragedy and with as much of the Reinhardt mob spirit as could be accommodated on their stage. . . . Even in this interpretation the play has its moments of genuine excitement. Nevertheless, you cannot help but feel that most of Dr. Schnitzler's finest gibes were buried under the falling of an uncommonly noisy Bastille.

# LATER FULL-LENGTH PLAYS

*The Veil of Beatrice*
(Der Schleier der Beatrice)

Arthur Schnitzler had begun his literary career writing verse dramas. *Ägidius* and his earliest printed dramatic attempt *Alkandi's Song* (*Alkandis Lied*), with their themes of fidelity, dream, and the confrontation of poet and ruler, already foreshadow *The Veil of Beatrice*. Of the one-act plays written prior to *The Veil of Beatrice*, only *Paracelsus* had been in verse. Subsequent verse dramas include the flashback scene in *The Lady with the Dagger* (blank verse), *The Big Wurstel Puppet Theater* (various verse forms), and, among the works of his later period, *The Sisters, or Casanova in Spa: Three Acts in One* and the five-act play *The Walk to the Pond* (both in blank verse). All of these dramas are important in terms of Schnitzler's work, but because he forced them into verse form, none of them enjoyed a very long life on the stage.

> For this is what it means to live: to be
> manifoldly entangled in a net,
> which is constantly expanding as every
> moment spins new threads for us.

These two verses of Schnitzler (published in 1895 in the *Wiener Allgemeine Zeitung*) could stand as the motto of *The Veil of Beatrice*. For the theme of the play is life, on which all of the dreams and deeds of the characters have been focused since they became threatened by death.

Schnitzler follows a characteristic of the time and leads us—as, before him, Hofmannsthal did in *Yesterday* and, after him, Thomas Mann in *Fiorenza*—into the Renaissance, which, because of the influence of Jacob Burckhardt and Nietzsche, was thought of as a world of heightened feelings and fame, of splendor and art, a world of intensified life and the presence of death. Festive verses and luxurious language, costuming, and stage setting provide the strange and precious frame for an occurrence that treats Schnitzler's typical problems and configurations in a form that he had not attempted previously: the form of the Shakespearean drama. There are a multitude of characters, five-act construction, blank verse, artful alternation between sober prose and the pathos of speech in verse, and, in addition, numerous details —from the eulogy over Filippo's body to the conclusion of the final act in heroic couplet.

Schnitzler himself described the genesis of this

play, which he worked on from the beginning of 1898 until the end of 1899. It began with this idea: "A bride wants to commit suicide with her lover. He dies and she, losing her courage at the last moment, flees, forgetting her veil. Because she is expected at home, she must climb the stairs once again in order to retrieve her veil from the dead man's room."

Only after this idea had been incorporated in Schnitzler's short story *The Dead Are Silent* (*Die Toten schweigen*) and had been performed as a pantomine, *The Veil of Pierette* (*Der Schleier der Pierrette*), was the first sketch developed into a historical drama that was set in Vienna around 1800:

> This decision resulted less from inner necessity and an actual connection between the characters and the subject matter on the one hand and time and place on the other, than from a certain inclination to believe that the characters would best live their lives to the fullest in this atmosphere.
>
> The play was carried out according to the new plan up to the middle of the second act. But here the following happens: one of the figures appears to cast off his mask in a mysterious manner, or rather, the intuitive power of the author (in this instance this statement is not intended as an artistic evaluation but only as a description of the psychological process) enables him to transform this figure through its ennobled language and actions into a character, who from this moment on is also

subject to the laws of human truth and reveals himself for what he really is, a prince of the Renaissance.

The main figure remains schematic longest, yet from the beginning she harbors within her the inclination to place herself in the middle of the circle of characters as a force that is unconscious, elemental, and extremely female.

The thought emerging from the plot: the embodiment of the feminine genius wavers between the man of action and the man of contemplation and would have to meet these two principles united in one man in order to rise to the possibility of fidelity. This idea, which is now exploited consciously and capriciously, illuminates the entire work from within.

This figure, despite whatever my reflection and intuition could come up with, nevertheless still lacked real life until by chance—during the very summer in which this work was written—the author encountered a woman who in many respects provided living insights into this literary figure. In behavior, physiognomy, gestures, and looks, the figure approaches closer and closer to the living individual. As a result, she becomes increasingly understandable to the author, and thus finally completed her development into a character.

The action is compressed into one day. Bologna will be stormed in twenty-four hours by the besieger, Cesare Borgia. Every individual trapped in the city must make a decision. He can try to flee (as do Filippo and Vittorino), prepare for battle and make his last will and testament (as Fran-

cesco, Beatrice's brother, does), or he can plunge
with complete abandon into a final orgy. Concentrated effort or abandonment in ecstasy—there
are no other possibilities. A finale of life begins, the
terminal point of which is foreseeable. This night
will be followed by eternal night. The agony of a
city is mirrored in the behavior of all of its
inhabitants: the same fate awaits courtiers and arti-
sans, aristocrats and soldiers, artists and courtesans. With catastrophe imminent, every action
becomes significant, every gesture a symbol of
human behavior. The Duke's notary, Cosini, expresses this idea, that now "every yes and no becomes a sign, and signifies more than itself."

The poet Filippo Loschi lives in the seclusion of
his garden (comparable to the gardens of Claudio
in Hofmannsthal's *Death and the Fool* and Titian
in his *The Death of Titian*). A wall separates the
secluded, introspective world of the artist from
political reality. Yet now, because his voluntary
isolation is turning into captivity endangering his
life, he rebels. Just as he did not participate in a
common life, he does not want to have to participate in a common death. When, three days before,
he had found Beatrice he had decided to renounce
fame, honor, and moral obligations, and to begin
a new life with her. But he is too much imprisoned
in himself to be able to live with her. He considers
her his own creation, and when she does not meet
the expectations of unconditional fidelity, which
he demands from her as his creation, he repudiates

her and tries to find a deeper experience in music and with courtesans. His three attempts to live fail: the contemplative life has failed because of external danger; the life with Beatrice fails because of his unconditional demands; the enjoyment of the moment fails because of his disenchantment. Suicide remains as the only possible deed of the free will: "To die of one's own will is freedom, and me thinks it to be the only freedom granted to us mortals!"

Beatrice stands at the center of the drama. Everything is related to her, the figures are grouped around her in concentric circles. Everything leads back to her, and the important problems of the play have their point of reference in her. She appears alternately to be a powerful sorceress or an ingenuous exalted saint. Her true nature, however, cannot be comprehended by such concepts as sorceress, prostitute, or saint, which do not adequately characterize her. On this point the theater critic and poet Alfred Polgar remarked: "Nobody knows women, not even Arthur Schnitzler, who knows them minutely."

Filippo had led Beatrice out of her puppetlike, uncommitted existence into a life of involvement. During this last night she wanders in despair along the boundaries set for her by destiny. Her fate exceeds her strength, for although so young, she is already fatigued. The events of this night greatly weary her. In a dream she had seen herself as the wife of the Duke, and thus she experienced her destiny in advance. Now she reports her dream to

Filippo, who interprets it as her desire to be unfaithful. He casts her out. Beatrice had not accepted her dream as a wish and had not interpreted it as a possibility. But what was only a
dream for Beatrice is for Filippo, who is a knowl-
edgeable interpreter of dreams, "desire without
courage." He could cope with facts but not with
possibilities or hidden wishes. (*The Veil of Beatrice* was written before Freud's *The Interpretation of Dreams*). On the basis of his interpretation
of her dream he feels that he has the right to re-
pudiate her. She dared to dream her own dream,
and therefore she is not Filippo's creation—one
more bitter realization for him in his existence that
abounds in thoughts and illusions. Dream actuality
is for him unassailable reality. The thought that
makes the dream more horrible than an actual
event is not that it could become reality, but that it
could become *possible*. Filippo rejects Beatrice out
of injured vanity. He wanted to develop her possibilities, wanted to make them into necessities,
which were to be determined by his creative
power.

Filippo does not know that by his rejection he
has paved the way for the fulfillment of Beatrice's
dream. But later, hardly married, Beatrice returns
to Filippo, wearing the veil that binds her to the
Duke. She drops the veil, symbol of her marital
fidelity. Thus, she releases herself from the Duke
and from the splendor, brilliance, and richness that
is hers as the Duchess. So far everything has pro-

ceeded as in a dream, and now she wants to glide from this beautiful dream into a beautiful death. Yet when she sees death threatening in its true form, she awakens. She is unable to take the poison and to die beside Filippo. Instead, she flees.

Just as the Duke and Filippo stand in relation to life, so they stand in relation to Beatrice, who is in the middle—beautiful, mysterious, fateful, but also fatal. The Duke does not think about Beatrice; he controls her existence as he is accustomed to commanding the fullness of life. Filippo knows only the momentary ecstasy, an intensification of life that has a claim to eternity. By contrast, life for the Duke is an even stream; he experiences the rich life, a life that is its own fulfillment. For Filippo, the artist who is placed on a level with Virgil and Petrarch, the question is whether he can unite with life through his art. He has to answer this question in the negative. Even poetry written on the basis of experience is still a substitute for life. The life that is not lived is mourned in a poem that produces pleasure for others. This realization drives the poet to self-destruction. After he sent Beatrice away, the discrepancy between life and literature became clear to Filippo: "And if out of this foolishness a song results, that is the highest prize that life throws to me for the disgrace that I am too weak to live my life with pride."

Filippo cannot leave his garden. The Duke on the other hand is a master in dealing with life.

What Filippo cannot handle with self-control the Duke handles with dignity. Chance ideas and circumstances, which Filippo cannot manage, are accepted by the Duke in a superior and casual manner. He rules while Filippo broods. The Duke is not aware of the miraculous; Filippo destroys it for himself. Both make unconditional demands. The Duke reaches into the infinite desired by Filippo, who envies him. The Duke finds it possible to compress his complete authority and life force into one moment, into one action. He is impetuous but not without mildness. An aesthete who also tortures— a Renaissance prince. He stands behind everything that he does with the full force of his personality. When he postulates beauty, it means without doubt that morality and legality have been canceled out in the face of death. It does not, however, signify anarchy but a reversal of the law. Aesthetic immorality is not only defended and practiced but is also elevated to binding law. Filippo provides the Duke with the philosophical tools that he needs: man is subject to eternal laws, but such determinism does not involve guilt; youth, beauty, and happiness are positive values, not gifts of hell. By this reasoning aesthetic immorality is defended as determinism. What Filippo seeks and the Duke accomplishes, namely, to compress all of life into one moment, leads to the view that even fidelity is only a momentary whim.

The play shows no development of the characters. Instead, they grow tired from their conflicts with one another and mature to a readiness for death. Filippo dies alone and in despair. Beatrice seeks peace of mind in death. The Duke alone rises above death! Through the fullness of his life he conquers death.

Contemporary judgment concerning *The Veil of Beatrice* is mixed. Max Koch considers the work "one of the most significant creations" from the period at the turn of the century. Rainer Maria Rilke, in a letter to Schnitzler, gave the following judgment: "The complicated nature of Beatrice is conceived in a wonderfully simple manner, and with truly great justice you stand above her and her confusions." Critics such as Polgar, Alfred Kerr, and Max Lorenz sensed the cool distance that emanates from the work. In their opinion the work is interesting but not gripping. Otto Brahm felt "more captivated than warmed." Here Schnitzler wanted to force, by means of grand gestures, what he achieved easily in his apparently undemanding melodies of love and death: "Schnitzler wanted to become Shakespeare, but in the attempt only ceased being Schnitzler," said Max Lorenz in his review of 1901.

•   •

The history of *The Veil of Beatrice* on the stage is not free of rejections, scandals, protests, and anti-Semitic attacks. In 1900 the premiere failed in

Breslau. In 1903 Otto Brahm performed it at the Deutsches Theater in Berlin. In 1911 the play appeared in the repertory in Hamburg.

It was not until 23 May 1925 that it was given for the first time in the Burgtheater in Vienna, where it remained in the repertory until 18 June 1926. After the director of the Burgtheater had first delayed his acceptance of the play and then rejected the work in 1900, the critics, Max Burckhard above all, demanded a Viennese performance. In the *Neue Freie Presse* of 24 May 1924 Raoul Auernheimer wrote that it is the most "Schnitzlerian work" because it is the most "poetic" drama. He explained the "Viennese prejudice" against the play by commenting that it does not take place in Vienna as one had come to expect of Schnitzler's dramas.

*The Lonely Way*
(Der einsame Weg)

*The Lonely Way*, a drama in five acts, is the first of Schnitzler's great dramas that are composed of scenes of conversational exchanges. The destinies of the characters bring them together for a short time, the paths of their lives cross and separate again—each is on his own lonely path.

Many years before the time of the play, Gabriele, who was then about to be married to Wegrat, had met and fallen in love with the painter Julian Fichtner. She had begged Fichtner to run away with her before her wedding day, but he had refused and they never saw each other again. When she married Wegrat, Gabriele was already expecting a child as a result of her brief affair with Fichtner.

The play opens just before the death of Gabriele. The action of the play centers around Felix, Gabriele's oldest child. Now a young man, Felix discovers that Fichtner, and not Wegrat, is his father. Fichtner, who has lived the life of a selfish egoist, wishes at last to establish a close bond with his son. Felix, however, turns from him to Wegrat, the father he has always known and loved as his own.

Sala, a middle-aged poet who, like Fichtner, has always lived a selfish life, points out to Fichtner that he has no right to his son. Because both Fichtner and Sala himself have lived only for themselves, they are free but condemned to a "lonely way."

Johanna, Felix's half-sister, meets and has an affair with Sala. She grows to love him deeply but refuses to marry him—she knows that he is the victim of a fatal illness and does not have long to live. When Sala learns that Johanna has drowned herself for his sake, he, too, commits suicide. Felix and Wegrat remain as the only ones who are not destined to a lonely way.

The lonely way of the characters represents not only the final outlook of the drama but is clearly evident even at the beginning. The period of harmonious agreement is over for the siblings Johanna and Felix. The idyl of mutual understanding lies in their childhood. Death as a premonition stands between them. The theme of death is brought into the play by Johanna. She has a presentiment about the death of her mother and knows about Sala's impending death, a death that she chooses to share with him when he asks her to share his life. The joint way into death is contrasted to the joint way into the future, which Felix and Wegrat will follow.

The interconnections between characters are many, and the most obvious is that of two groups, one of which is centered around Johanna, the other around Felix. The first group includes Dr. Reumann and his patient Sala, in their efforts to win Johanna; the second includes Wegrat and Fichtner. Gabriele, as the mother of Johanna and Felix, is the link between the two groups. Wegrat and Reumann, the painter-professor and the physician, are the only ones who lead an active life, as contrasted to the two artists Sala and Fichtner, the

poet and the painter. In the artistic sphere Irene
Herms, an actress and former mistress of Fichtner,
stands between the two: she recited Sala's verses in
the theater and was Fichtner's model. Only
through Felix does Fichtner now stand in any relationship to Gabriele. The relationship between Dr.
Reumann and Sala is that of the physician who
knows about the impending death of his patient.

Julian Fichtner tries to leave his lonely way by
creating a bond between himself and his son. But
even though he hopes until the conclusion of the
play, for a life shared with Felix, he must continue
his lonely way to the end. Gabriele dies in the dis-
consolate loneliness of a lifelong lie. She has en-
trusted her secret only to her physician, Dr. Reumann. Wegrat has never suspected that he is not
Felix's father. He is not aware of his own loneliness: the fact that he knows nothing about the lie
that has darkened Gabriele's life has made his family life secure. He also knows nothing of Johanna's
attachment to Sala and therefore cannot understand her death.

Irene Herms, recently retired from the theater,
has her lonely way ahead of her. It can only be a
sad one because she has not found the fulfillment
that would have enabled her to establish a binding
commitment to life: a child had been denied to
her. Fichtner's portrait of her shows her in the
loneliness of an actress whose life is centered on
the theater. Without a child nothing remains but

phantoms. For the actress a child would represent more than just an offspring; it would represent a rescue from a life of mere appearance, an undeniable reality, a confirmation of her own reality joined with life through the duty of motherhood. Therefore, even marriage holds only secondary importance for her. More than anyone else in the play, Professor Wegrat knows and fulfills his duties to his children. He, too, knows to what extent resignation is part of the responsibilities.

What in Fichtner's case is the loneliness that resulted from a misunderstanding of his youthful freedom (freedom that, with youth fading, transforms into yearning for tranquility and human bonds) is, in the case of Sala, self-imposed loneliness of the spirit, the highest level of consciousness. Sala's love for Johanna does not increase his human stature. His proposal of marriage and his intimated resolve to end his life by his own hand, however, are at least moments that allow him to overcome his loneliness. Now the aging Sala experiences what Fichtner in his youth had once considered himself worthy of—a girl who would take her own life for his sake. Fichtner loses all his illusions; Sala has none to lose. Fichtner's arrogant ego stands between himself and reality, while it is intellect that stands between Sala and reality. While this distance from reality is too great with Sala, Johanna is too oppressively close to the destinies of the people around them.

Sala identifies with the young people as no one else here. He intends to take Felix on his planned research expedition to Baktria. The only person marked for death lives in a youthful manner, while Fichtner and Irene Herms descend the path into old age. If Sala is the catalyst of the play, stimulating the young people to act for themselves, Fichtner is the author, the puppeteer, and Gabriele, Wegrat, and Herms, his marionettes. The interconnections between characters extend into the infinite. After rereading the play in 1912, Schnitzler noted: "It is on the whole, it almost seems to me, of a novel spiritual intensity."

·   ·

*The Lonely Way* is an example of the fact that only through the efforts of ensemble work, in the interplay of acting achievements, can one do justice to Arthur Schnitzler's dramas. Neither the guest theater of the turn of the century nor the star theater of the present can exhaust their wealth of relationships and linguistic nuances. Schnitzler has written great, coveted roles, but they must not be taken as virtuoso parts. Performance of these roles must always fit into the framework of the play and of the ensemble. For decades Albert Bassermann made guest appearances as Sala on German stages and thus kept *The Lonely Way* in the repertory. The famous theater critic Julius Bab wrote that Sala was presented as: "the aristocratic outsider, the completely aesthetic spectator, the exclusive hedonist who gives nothing of himself and who with approaching age slowly freezes in his cold majesty." But Schnitzler and his play did not come off well in such a performance. In the same breath Bab writes that the play was "not without poetic value, but for all that it was so weak theatrically, so poor in external action, that it remains a wonder how Bassermann could bring this role to a great and lasting success."

The Sala of our time is Leopold Rudolf, who played the role, in Vienna (1962–63) and Hamburg (1966) under Heinrich Schnitzler's direction, not as star but always within the ensemble alongside equally capable performers. Leopold Rudolf's Sala does not lose his arrogance over the sacrifice of Johanna, but his aloofness from other people is not without mildness, and his consciousness of approaching death makes him not only supercilious but also nervous.

*The Lonely Way* was first performed on 13 February 1904 at the Deutsches Theater in Berlin. At the Burgtheater it was in the repertory from 19 February 1914 to 10 April 1919, though not often performed. In the United States it was offered, in 1931, in an adaptation by Philip Moeller, presented by the Theater Guild at the National Theater in Washington, D. C. In Germany in recent times *The Lonely Way* has been performed in Baden-Baden and Hamburg (1966–67).

## Intermezzo
(Zwischenspiel)

Schnitzler subtitled this play "Comedy in Three Acts." A conductor, Amadeus Adams, and his wife, the singer Cäcilie Ortenburg, have made a mutual agreement that their marriage will be based on truth. Thus they confess that in the course of time they have grown apart from one another. In a rational manner they pursue this revelation to its logical conclusion and decide to remain good friends. But their relationship based on friendship is destroyed in one night of re-awakened passion for one another. Now their marriage is no longer possible on any basis, for during the preceding period of freedom, they both had deceived each other—he in reality, and she in thought. They have to separate. Not until twenty years later, in *Rhapsody: A Dream Novel* (*Traumnovelle*), does Schnitzler describe a possible reconciliation.

Schnitzler has written a play full of tenderness and, at the same time, hopelessness, a play about marriage full of despair and inexorability. In *The Lonely Way* it has shown that, in the long run, man cannot live and does not want to live, a lonely life. In *Intermezzo* it becomes clear that even marriage cannot possibly endure for long if the partners do not dedicate themselves with all their will to their mutual life together.

.   .

Amadeus, the leading male role of *Intermezzo*, was one of the most praised accomplishments of Josef Kainz, one of Austria's best-known stage actors. This play remained in the repertory of Vienna's Burgtheater from its premiere in 1905 until 1919.

*The Call of Life*
(Der Ruf des Lebens)

This "Drama in Three Acts" consists rather of three one-act plays on the life of Marie Moser. In the first act Marie suffers and murders, in the second act she loves, and in the third she renounces life. Because of his will to live, Marie's

father, who had been an officer in the cavalry, had
fled in the face of the enemy, which has left him
with a lost battle on his conscience. Now, before
the next campaign, the members of his old regiment have sworn an oath to expiate this retreat by
their death. Thus Moser becomes the murderer of
the young men in the regiment. His cowardice,
however, is only the outward cause for the oath.
The real reason is that the colonel, who has pur-
posely roused the men to such fervor, wants to
take revenge on this regiment because his wife has
deceived him with one of the officers. Marie loves
this same officer and wants to be with him during
the last night before the departure of the troop.
When her father tries to prevent her from leaving,
she kills him.

The drama leads into the depths of human problems. It shows man's behavior toward life—not toward the conditions of existence, toward possibilities, or the workings of fate—but toward life itself,
life that is always finite, always terminated by
men. This life takes its course in time, but its significance extends beyond the temporal. It is made
into an idol. It becomes objectified, it is there just
outside Marie's window. Life does not mean
breathing and functioning physically, but adven-
turous experience. At first Marie does not understand experience as the conventional dedication of
a nurse (which she becomes in the third act), but
as ecstatic abandon. This urge to self-surrender is

understood as the call of life and as freedom, not as a compulsion of instinct.

Regarding this play, Schnitzler noted in 1912: "Despite beautiful features of great quality the play as a whole is a failure. Some possibilities for saving it have occurred to me." He died in 1931 while revising this play.

·   ·

*The Call of Life* was not received in friendly fashion by the critics at its premiere in Berlin at the Lessingtheater on 24 February 1906. The new version that Schnitzler was working on was to have been performed, according to Sol Liptzin, whose book on Arthur Schnitzler was published in 1932, by Max Reinhardt on Schnitzler's seventieth birthday.

*The Young Medardus*
(Der junge Medardus)

Schnitzler wrote *The Young Medardus* in time for the hundredth anniversary of the battle of Aspern in the wars between Napoleon and Austria.

This work is a "Dramatic History with a Prologue and Five Acts." It is Schnitzler's longest drama and contains a wide range of individually character-ized persons.

Like *The Green Cockatoo*, *The Young Medardus* develops out of the existing historical situation, which in addition to providing the background is intrinsic to the plot. The image of Napoleon is mir-rored in the characters, precisely because he does not appear in person.

The young Medardus had set out to seek re-venge on the French for the death of his father. He does not accomplish this, for a more recent mis-fortune in his family takes precedence over the tragedy of many years past. His sister and the emi-grant François, the heir to the French throne, have drowned themselves in the Danube because the Duke of Valois would not tolerate their marriage, this misalliance with a commoner. The Valois pre-tend that they are continuing to maintain their court in Vienna, they keep alive the illusion of rul-ing. Medardus now believes that he must take a new revenge—on the Valois.

The proper form for requiting his father's death would have been to enter the struggle against Na-poleon. The proper form of revenge for the death of his sister is love. Medardus plans to pretend to fall in love with Helene, the sister of François, in order to sacrifice her to scandal after he seduces her. But Medardus is a dreamer: he cannot play-act or dissemble or deceive. What he had planned to have end with the seduction of Helene develops into genuine love. Their affair culminates in deception by Helene, whom Medardus believes to be on her way to a liaison with Napoleon, the victor in Schönbrunn. For a third time Medardus prepares himself for revenge, this time for himself and with success. He kills Helene on her way to Napoleon, whom she was actually planning to assassinate. Thus, Medardus at the end of his journey becomes the rescuer of Napoleon, whose mortal enemy he had sworn himself to be at the beginning of his course of action. He disdains Napoleon's offer to reward him for his deed, openly declares himself Napoleon's enemy, and does not resist execution by a firing squad.

The German literary scholar Friedrich Blume called *The Young Medardus* a "comedy of the heroic; not heroes fill the stage but comedians and their public." Medardus always acts differently than he had planned, but always as he wants. He always lives in the presence of his true feelings. Fate has determined him to be a clown precisely because these feelings contradict each other. Instead of a positive deed he achieves only an act of violence. He elevates this act, however, to a deed worthy of his death by belatedly making Helene's intention to kill Napoleon his own intention. Thus, he returns to the intention with which he had set out.

*The Young Medardus* was one of the repertory plays of the Burgtheater from its premiere on 24 November 1910 until 1932. In 1932 Franz Herte-rich directed a new production. The Burgtheater was less fortunate with a revival of the drama under the direction of Adolf Rott in the 1962–63 season.

## *The Vast Domain*
(Das weite Land)

In *The Lonely Way* there was a complexity of relationships between the characters with no single influence playing a predominant role. *Intermezzo* involved two people and their marriage; each of the two at various times was tied to another person, with whom he deceived or wished to deceive his spouse. In *The Vast Domain* the manufacturer Hofreiter plays the main role, and all of the other characters stand in a relationship to him. All other characters are only there either to be controlled by him or to serve as a foil for his way of life.

*The Vast Domain* is a tragicomedy about the impulse to dominate. A man compels society to play a comedy with him but not against him—for then he makes use of the social conventions to kill his antagonist in a duel. Comedy turns into tragicomedy.

Hofreiter has a faithful wife in Genia. This seems uncanny to him, for while her faithfulness is appropriate to the convention of bourgeois marriage, it does not correspond to the rules of the social game. The social game sanctifies the fiction of fidelity, but not fidelity itself. Fidelity is inhuman. People live beside one another in marriage, not with one another. Thus, when Genia enters into the game and deceives her husband with Lieutenant Otto, Hofreiter no longer needs to feel guilty toward his wife. But he does not want to put up with this, and instead reinvokes the bourgeois convention. He challenges the young lieutenant to a duel, in which he kills him.

People have entered into the game. They drift, act as if they could not behave differently, and, like the hotel director Aigner, justify their conduct by saying that the soul is a "vast domain." Thus, one cannot be held responsible for one's behavior. Schnitzler's title is ironic. The characters, who eagerly seize upon this phrase and use it as an excuse, unmask themselves in the process.

Schnitzler created a moral counterbalance in the figure of the actress Anna Meinhold, the divorced wife of Aigner and the mother of Lieutenant Otto. She is the measure of human behavior. Her marriage foundered on the uncompromising nature of her love. She would not forgive her husband's infidelity, though it would have been convenient. She makes a clear distinction between the stage and life, and in life she does not play the game of the others. Knowing all the variations, she does not show herself in any of them; she remains the most responsible and honorable person. These characteristics also determine her relationship to Genia, and it is because of Genia that she loses her son.

· ·

*The Vast Domain* was premiered simultaneously in nine theaters on 14 October 1911. The Viennese premiere was staged by Hugo Thimig, who also played the hotel porter. In the period up to 26 January 1919 the drama was part of the repertory of the Burgtheater. In 1959 Ernst Lothar produced a revival of the tragicomedy.

In 1964 *The Vast Domain* was given a production in Hamburg. After this performance Henning Rischbieter made the following comment in *Theater heute* (Vol. 5, No. 12) about the principal character, Hofreiter:

> Socialite, gentleman, lover, woman chaser, nervy and nervous, vehement and powerful, unbelieving and full of feeling, self-confident, and yet at the mercy of himself: the European bourgeois of the

best type, titanic and self-destructive, on the eve of, and with a premonition of, World War I, with the destruction of himself and his class imminent.

In 1967 *The Vast Domain* was performed in Hanover.

## *Professor Bernhardi*

The question of whether one, by administering last rites, should be permitted to disturb the euphoria of a young girl patient who does not know that she is going to die is answered in the negative by Professor Bernhardi, the Jewish director of the Elisabethinum clinic in Vienna at the turn of the century. In this single instance he refuses to allow the priest summoned by the nurse Sister Ludmilla to see the patient.

Bernhardi can justify his act to himself. He made this decision according to his conscience and his own judgment, believing that he was making easier the last moments of this patient. But his behavior in this particular case turns out badly for him. His intention failed. Sister Ludmilla announced the priest to the dying girl and thus made her aware of her real condition. Her death was hastened because of this. When the incident is brought before the public, it is distorted into an interference with religion. Envy and anti-Semitic politics are given the opportunity to proceed against the successful doctor. The patrons of the clinic withdraw, and Bernhardi's enemies in the institute become emboldened, while his friends misunderstand his action as an attempt to set a precedent. He is suspended from his position at the clinic, is brought to trial, and must go to prison.

Unexpectedly, the esteemed Professor Bernhardi, the personal physician of the royal family and a friend of a current cabinet member, has been pushed down the social ladder to the lowest step. Yet, hardly has he been released from prison when public opinion changes again. Bernhardi, who throughout the entire period has wanted only to be able to return as soon as possible to the undisturbed practice of his profession, is rehabilitated and becomes the hero of the day.

Bernhardi stands alone. Nobody rescues him. He is surrounded by ambitious or opportunistic men (for example, Hochroitzpointner, whose testimony at the trial had helped to convict Bernhardi), scoundrels, and fools, as Bernhardi's colleague Dr. Pflugfelder characterizes them.

Bernhardi is not a martyr, which is what Löwenstein, another of Bernhardi's colleagues, would like to make of him. For Bernhardi it is not a question of conviction but solely of truthfulness and correct behavior, which are determined only on the basis of reason and morality. Bernhardi can be objective because he is responsible only to himself. Thus, he is in a different position than the priest, who would not be able to answer to the church if he were to do only what he personally thinks and considers to be correct.

It is inevitable that Bernhardi come into conflict with a conservative, church-influenced society (the religious arguments are supported by racist, nationalistic prejudices), for those who envy Bernhardi, knowing exactly what they are doing, have the basis of their support in this social order. The confrontation between the duty of the physician (to judge the condition and to relieve the suffering of the individual patient) and the duty of the priest (to administer religious consolation to every Christian) is not the theme of the drama, but only the catalyst for a play that concerns anti-Semitism in a Christian society. A spark is struck and ignites an explosion. Behind the mask of Christianity are concealed corruption, envy, and human stupidity that the individual cannot surmount. This is a small anti-Semitic scandal, nothing world-shaking to be sure, but the repercussions are great enough to alert the public to the consequences that could possibly result.

In this drama the evil spirits are banished once

more. But when Schnitzler wrote *Professor Bernhardi* between 1910 and 1912, Adolf Hitler was already promoting anti-Semitism in Vienna, and we know the consequences of that drama. Now that Schnitzler's fears have been proved justified, *Professor Bernhardi* produces an even stronger effect today. Everything turns out well, and even the petty culprits are punished. But the truly guilty individuals remain in office, and the Hochroitzpointners of this world developed into the practitioners of euthanasia.

Balance is restored once more between the personal and public spheres, but already there is an abyss, which a generation later can no longer be bridged.

The Jewish problem in all of the variations that are presented in the play also symbolizes general ones: the position of a truthful, honorable man in society; the determination of the conduct of the individual by the conventions of the others; the problem ultimately of free will. Bernhardi himself points out this last issue—it became the theme of a philosophical treatise he had begun to write while in prison.

The problem of free will found an apparent solution in society: the social game. By this means, opportune and corrupt behavior is concealed behind a mask of conformity to conventions and observance of rules, which make one comfortably free from the observance of such moral commandments as responsibility, truthfulness, and genuineness. This game (which is not deception because everyone is aware that all are wearing masks that they drop when talking to Bernhardi in private conversation) reveals the breach between the private and public spheres, between understanding and confessing, between human and political behavior. Everyone except Bernhardi plays a role, and if he wants to escape unscathed, he, too, will have to join in the game. There are different roles. For the minor players society has created the choruses, the political parties, which engage one either for or against. If he does not want to conform politically, the individual is powerless and runs amok against the social system. Dr. Pflugfelder, in the role of the antagonist, agrees with his opponents that there is a Bernhardi "case" and that even the patient herself represents a "case" (that it is not simply a matter of a physician and a human being).

The cabinet member, who lives not for the sake of a cause but for the game, is juxtaposed with those who become involved. Where the others are decent supernumeraries, he is the great actor who has the public in his hand but who, for the effectiveness that is more important to him than the content of his speech, adapts to the slightest wish of his public. In society, which a stage where false emotions conceal egotistical purposes, one must be a cabinet member. A less exposed and thus less endangered position is held by Counselor Winkler. He is the only one who knows about the game and observes it from his secure position.

Even in the future Bernhardi will not observe the rules of the social game. He will continue to oppose ideology and egotism with his duty as a physician and his sense of responsibility. He is and remains a man among puppets.

. .

*Professor Bernhardi* was premiered on 28 November 1912 at the Kleines Theater in Berlin. Otto Brahm had declined to accept the play on the grounds that the problems treated in the drama did not exist in Protestant Berlin. Nevertheless, it was a success at its premiere there. The Deutsches Volkstheater in Vienna had sought permission to perform the play on 13 January 1913 but was given a negative decision on 25 January 1913:

> Even if the reservations that exist against the performance of the work, from the standpoint of protecting the religious feelings of the population, could be eliminated by cuts or by making a number of textual changes, nevertheless the play in its total construction, through the collective effect of the episodes that have been brought together to illustrate our public life, represents Austrian state institutions with manifold distortions of the national conditions in such a deprecating fashion, that its performance on a stage in our country cannot, in order to protect the public's interests, be permitted. In the face of this objec-

tion the literary importance of this play cannot be taken into account as the deciding factor in the question of its performance.

The Deutsches Volkstheater did finally perform *Professor Bernhardi* in 1918, after the collapse of the monarchy and, with it, the censorship bureau. Heinrich Schnitzler staged an English-language performance in New York in 1936.

For twenty years the role of Bernhardi has been identified with Ernst Deutsch. In 1946 he played Bernhardi in the Renaissancebühne in Vienna, in 1955 under Heinrich Schnitzler in Berlin, and since 1965 at the Burgtheater.

Heinrich Schnitzler also staged *Professor Bernhardi* in Stuttgart on 10 November 1964. A television performance of Heinrich Schnitzler's version has been made by Erich Neuburg.

*Fink and Fliederbusch*

Approximately a hundred years before Schnitzler wrote his three-act comedy on the theme of journalists, the German political economist Adam Müller proposed to the Prussian government that he would undertake the publishing of a newspaper that "on the one hand would be overtly under the authority of the state council and favorable to the government, and on the other hand, anonymously and under the same cover, would represent the public's point of view. In other words, he intended to write a government and an opposition newspaper at the same time." And in October 1919, two years after the first performance of *Fink and Fliederbusch*, there was the case of a spy in Berlin who, under a different name, gave evidence against himself. Examples of such fickleness and double identities could be multiplied.

Schnitzler wrote a play about the fickleness of journalists. The journalist as a comedian of truth can represent one thing without denying another. He can convince without believing. Truth is a role that he assumes and that he can exchange, with one limitation: "If somebody plays a role, he has a responsibility to carry it out consistently." Fliederbusch, a reporter for the serious literary and political newspaper *Die Gegenwart*, writes also for the fashionable society magazine *Die elegante Welt* under the name Fink. The situation is pushed to absurdity by the particular vehemence with which Fink and Fliederbusch feud, until they have to challenge each other to a duel. Along with the question of truthfulness, the play presents the question of identity. Who is who? The day before yesterday, Fliederbusch, yesterday Fink, today both or perhaps neither of the two."

### *The Sisters, or Casanova at Spa*
(Die Schwestern, oder Casanova in Spa)

*The Sisters, or Casanova at Spa*, subtitled "A Comedy in Verse," contains "three acts in one" and deals with love, deception, and fidelity. "Through the play of chance a young man one night embraces, not the lady who promised him her favor, but another woman who was not expecting him."

Casanova, who failed to notice the exchange of partners, answers the question of who was deceived: "All three were deceived, each in his own way: the man doubly, the women once. Thus everything was balanced out, and I declare the whole adventure invalid."

In Casanova's opinion, the only certainty in love that may be designated as fidelity is the return. The dancer Teresa returns to him. "She returned to me. That alone is fidelity."

## The Walk to the Pond
(Der Gang zum Weiher)

*The Walk to the Pond* is a political play involving war, emigration, and patriotism. Baron von Mayenau, a former chancellor, is called on for advice. The emperor, whose marshal is urging him into war with the neighboring country, is unsure whether or not to declare war. Mayenau accepts his old position as chancellor, hoping to prevent this war. But when he and the ambassador of the other country do come to an agreement, their messenger reaches the front lines too late—war has already begun.

The marshal's son, the patriotic soldier Konrad, is in love with Mayenau's daughter, Leonilda. But Konrad has a rival in Sylvester Thorn, Mayenau's friend of many years. Thorn had left the country some years before because of discriminatory practices against him and is now returning only to pick up an old diary he had left with Mayenau—he intends to return to his mistress, who is expecting a child. Instead, he falls in love with Leonilda and proposes to her. She, however, tells him to return to his "wife" and to come back to her only when he is sure he loves her. Thorn leaves, but he soon comes back to Leonilda when both his mistress and the child die in childbirth. Because he had actually wished for their deaths in order to be free for Leonilda, he is so overcome with guilt that he drowns himself in a pond near the Mayenau home. This "walk to the pond" is another lonely way.

## Comedy of Seduction
(Komödie der Verführung)

In all of his works Schnitzler tried to create man in all of his possibilities. In his later dramas he reduced his early structural principle to focusing on three people. This more concentrated, triangular constellation recurs constantly without constraining the action or restricting the meaning of the sentences. This structure, which begins with the division into acts, is continued in the style, and on into the final refinements of the characters' thoughts. Or rather, after he has once established structure as limitation and principle, Schnitzler does everything he can to loosen it again.

In the first act of *Comedy of Seduction*, the destiny of each of three Viennese women begins to take its course. Aurelie is the beautiful aristocrat, Judith is the wealthy bourgeois, and Seraphine is a violinist from a petty bourgeois family. Aurelie, who has promised to choose a husband from among three suitors at a masked ball, finally decides for Falkenir, a middle-aged widower. He, however, rejects her because he feels that she has not yet been exposed to the temptations of life and cannot, therefore, truly know herself.

The second act is in three scenes, and each of the three women has one of the scenes. Each woman awakens to self-consciousness, to her destiny, after she has been seduced by Max von Reisenberg, the son of a jeweler. Max emancipates each of these women to her real self.

The third act brings all the characters together again, at a resort hotel, on the day before the outbreak of World War I. Judith leaves on a yacht with young Prince Arduin, one of Aurelie's former suitors. Seraphine refuses to marry Max even though she is expecting his child. Falkenir is now urging Aurelie to marry him. After warning him of her "loose" life since his earlier rejection of her, Aurelie agrees. Instead of joining him, however, she takes a boat out on the water, and when

Falkenir follows her in another boat she jumps into the water. Falkenir jumps too and, in an embrace, they drown together.

As in Shakespeare's comedies there are couples but no heroes. The characters are held together by the structure of the play. The theme here is seduction. Seduction is an enticement to surrender, whether it be induced through atmospheric influences, through will, or through desire. The seducer is there; he does not need to exert his will, he needs only to be present. Aurelie does not want to be tempted. She wants to let herself be guided by Falkenir, whom she has selected from among her three suitors. She wants to rely on him and feel secure. Falkenir, however, believes that she must experience the possibilities of her life to the fullest so that she will know herself. According to his theory (he is a theorist), as long as there remains a possibility of being confronted by temptation, there remains an obligation toward life. Being seduced is the way to self-realization. After Aurelie has experienced all of the heights and depths of life, there remains for her only the union with Falkenir in death. Seduction is the multiforce in the drama, not its goal. Max shows the way. He is not present for the sake of seduction itself but acts as its catalyst. Through him each of the women fulfills her destiny: for Aurelie it is torment and ruin, for Judith acknowledgment of love, and for Seraphine motherhood.

The play is a comedy because all human activity is ridiculous in view of destiny, the mind's powerlessness about coping with destiny, war, vacillations of the soul, and the inability to resist temptations of every kind.

The society at the turn of the century plays its own comedy here for the last time. The princes and adventurers die out, and the pensioned actors (such as Eligius Fenz, Seraphine's father) no longer have any significance. They have finished their roles as the heroes of society.

. .

*Comedy of Seduction*, which Schnitzler completed on 1 August 1914, the day of the outbreak of World War I, was performed from its premiere at the Burgtheater on 11 October 1924 until 1927 under Hans Brahm's direction. During the Vienna Festival Weeks in 1966 Gustav Manker attempted a revival of *Comedy of Seduction* at the Deutsches Volkstheater in Vienna with little success. The structure of the play was no longer recognizable; the lightness of the drama sounded laborious, the seriousness tormented. A good performance would have to make clear the decline of Viennese society of all levels before World War I.

## In the Play of the Summer Breezes
(Im Spiel der Sommerlüfte)

Are we a plaything of every breath of air?
—GOETHE, *Faust I*

In this drama in three acts games begin and end without any consequences, remorse, or guilt. In the sultriness of an Indian summer, relationships or responsibilities are formed and dissolved. The game is no longer structured; one is sacrificed to a game over which one has no control. One is vulnerable and can only wait passively but ready to follow every temptation until a thunder storm ends everything.

*In the Play of the Summer Breezes* reflects the style of Schnitzler's late period, with its emphasis on little causes and great effects, which, however, carry no great consequences. The causes disappear and are attributed to its being summertime. The self dissolves into a state of flux; the self is not dependent on moods but on weather conditions.

## *The Word*
(Das Wort)

Rarely are the unpublished works in a writer's literary estate as rich as those of Schnitzler. Despite World War II and the emigration of his heirs, a vast number of notes, plans, and half-finished plays have been preserved. Schnitzler had always reworked his plays a number of times (*Hands Around* is one of a few exceptions) and carried them around with him for an extended period. He worked on the five-act tragicomedy *The Word*, one of the most extensive of the remaining fragments, from 1901 until 1931—that is, until just before his death. There are several drafts and many variants of individual scenes; the characters changed in the course of the years, and their contours became blurred.

The poet Anastasius Treuenhof (a character bearing a similarity to the Austrian writer Peter Altenberg) practically lives at a café. He is a gossip who understands the human soul but does not put any value on verbal communication. A young painter falls in love with the wife of a tailor. On Treuenhof's advice, the tailor gives up his wife. She, however, does not go along with the "either/or" attitude of the men but rather practices an amoral "not only . . . but also." This destroys the painter, who believes in true love. Treuenhof gives the already tottering man an extra shove with the reproach that he lacks the courage to kill himself. When Treuenhof later hears of the young man's suicide, he raves about him enthusiastically as one who remained true to the absolute. But when Treuenhof is himself invited to die in beauty by a sentimental female tourist, he becomes furious—he wants to live.

The naive ones go to ruin on words that come at the wrong time; the unreflecting care nothing for words. It is only a few who have sufficient sense of responsibility to reflect on what they say. "To use words in such a way as to lie as little as possible"—this was the advice Schnitzler wanted to convey in this drama. It remained a fragment.

. .

The fragments of *The Word* were published in book form in 1966, but they were badly arranged and not usable for the stage. In 1969 the Theater in der Josefstadt asked Friedrich Schreyvogl, a former director of the Burgtheater, to revise and make necessary additions to *The Word* to prepare it for a production. Ernst Haeusserman, also a former director of the Burgtheater, was asked to do the staging. The performance, which opened on 29 October, was a success. That the play was a fragment was not readily apparent—the edges had been polished over and the cracks covered. The performance made the play, and the play proved its value through a long run. It is doubtful that such a daring venture could be successfully repeated by a less brilliant company.

*March of the Shadows*
(Zug der Schatten)

It was Schnitzler's method to begin by determining in the sketches *what* his characters were going to say. *How* they would say it would be determined only in the course of the often interrupted development of the drama. In this way some scenes were rewritten as many as twenty times. *March of the Shadows*, on which Schnitzler worked from 1911 to 1930, was never finished. The nine scenes, which were to be joined into a kind of

MARCH OF THE SHADOWS | 189

society drama, somewhat in the manner of *Comedy of Seduction*, were never completed. Two plot lines were to be interconnected: the first is that of three middle-class girls who do not wish to tie down their husbands or friends, either out of a desire to be free themselves, or out of maternal resignation, or out of love. The second plot is that of a young actress who kills herself after her *second* lover, whom, in contrast to the first, she really loved, leaves her. Acting as intermediary between the two worlds—the bourgeois world and the theater world—is the dramatist Karl Bern, a typical Schnitzlerian "literateur," who likes to see himself as a manipulator of others' lives, sharpening conflicts by intrigue in order to observe psychological effects.

*March of the Shadows* is unfinished in that each of the figures is only a mouthpiece for his own theoretical opinion, not a real character. Most of the figures are shadows, but not as the word is used in the title (which was meant to suggest a train of reminiscences of Schnitzler's own pre-World War I characters). "And if you reject my heart in this hour, because you have never so little deserved it, I will offer it to you again anyway, because never have you needed this heart so much as now"—such sentences as this, such stilted and rhetorically empty banners of conviction would surely not have been allowed to stand in Schnitzler's final version.

The theatrical atmosphere, however, which is

half the play, is created with that rather exaggerated veracity familiar from Schnitzler's other plays. And not all of the characters in this fragment are mere diagrams. We have, for example, such characters as the bit player Dregulein. Ridiculed by his colleagues, turned into a masochist by years of humiliation, he asks the young actress to give up her humanity, too, in order to further her career. And he is malicious enough to tell the unpleasant truth. That he does so in a genial manner is satire: and in this Schnitzler imitated Johann Nestroy and anticipated another Austrian playwright, Ödön von Horváth.

. .

Vienna's Volkstheater did not attempt to revise the original material for its premiere of *March of the Shadows* on 19 December 1971. Gustav Manker's direction showed too much respect for the series of scenes as they were found in Schnitzler's rough draft—and faithfulness to the text when only a rough draft is involved is no virtue in the theater. It would have been possible to extract finished scenes and fragments out of the darkness of the whole. In this way, one would not have created the impression of a finished play, but neither would one have created the impression of a bad one.

# BIBLIOGRAPHY

## Works by Schnitzler

"Arthur Schnitzler: Briefe über das Theater." *Forum* 3, no. 34 (October 1956):366–69.

"Rainer Maria Rilke und Arthur Schnitzler: Ihr Briefwechsel." *Wort und Wahrheit* 13 (1958):283–98.

"Frühlingsnacht im Seziersaal: Phantasie." In *S. Fischer Almanach*, Year 76, pp. 12–17. Frankfurt, 1962.

*Hugo von Hofmannsthal-Arthur Schnitzler: Briefwechsel*. Edited by Therese Nickl and Heinrich Schnitzler. Frankfurt, 1964. Also "Letzter Brief an Hugo von Hofmannsthal." In *S. Fischer Almanach*, Year 80. Frankfurt, 1966.

"Kriegsgeschichte: Ein Entwurf." *Literatur und Kritik* 13 (April 1967):133f.

"Roman-Fragment." Edited by Reinhard Urbach. *Literatur und Kritik* 13 (April 1967):135–83.

"Novellette: Ein Entwurf." In *S. Fischer Almanach*, Year 82, pp. 53–61. Frankfurt, 1968.

*Jugend in Wien: Eine Autobiographie*. Edited by Therese Nickl and Heinrich Schnitzler. Vienna, Munich, and Zurich, 1968.

*Meistererzählungen*. Frankfurt, 1969.

*Frühe Gedichte*. Edited with introduction by Herbert Lederer. Berlin, 1969.

"Das Haus Delorme." Edited by Reinhard Urbach. In *Ver Sacrum*, pp. 46–55. Vienna, 1970.
"Aus Arthur Schnitzlers Werkstatt: Unveröffentlichte Entwürfe und Szenen." *Neue Zürcher Zeitung*, 7 February 1971, pp. 51f.
*Meisterdramen*. Frankfurt, 1971.

### COLLECTIONS

*Die erzählenden Schriften*. 2 vols. Frankfurt, 1961.
*Die dramatischen Werke*. 2 vols. Frankfurt, 1962.
*Aphorismen und Betrachtungen*. Edited by Robert O. Weiss. Frankfurt, 1967.

## English Translations of the Plays

*Anatol: A Sequence of Dialogues*. New York: M. Kennerley, 1911; and Boston: Little, Brown, 1916. Also: *The Affairs of Anatol: A Cycle of One-Act Plays*. New York: Samuel French, 1933; and "Anatol." In *From the Modern Repertoire: Series Three*, pp. 175–240. Edited by Eric Bentley. Bloomington: Indiana University Press, 1956.
*Countess Mizzi*. Boston: Little, Brown, 1907.
*Free Game*. Boston: Badger, 1913.
*Gallant Cassian: A Puppet Play in One Act*. Boston: Leroy Philipps, 1921.
*Hands Around: A Roundelay in Ten Dialogues*. New

York: Julian Press, 1929. Also: *Merry-Go-Round*. London: Weidenfeld & Nicholson, 1953; *La Ronde (Reigen)*. London: Harborough, 1959; *Dance of Love*. New York: Universal Publishing & Distributing Corp., 1965; and "La Ronde: Ten Dialogues." In *Masters of the Modern Drama*, pp. 245–69. Edited by Haskell M. Block and Robert G. Shedd. New York: Random House, 1962.

*Light-O'-Love: A Drama in Three Acts*. Chicago: Dramatic Publishing Co., 1912. Also: *Playing with Love*. Prologue by Hugo von Hofmannsthal. Chicago: A. C. McClurg, 1914.

*The Lonely Way*. Boston: Little, Brown, 1904; and New York: Rialto Service Bureau, 1931.

*Professor Bernhardi*. New York: Simon & Schuster, 1928. Also: *The Anti-Semites (Professor Bernhardi): A Play*. Girard, Kansas: Haldeman-Julius, 1920.

COLLECTIONS

*Anatol. Living Hours. The Green Cockatoo*. New York: The Modern Library, 1925.

*Comedies of Words, and Other Plays*. Cincinnati: Stewart & Kidd, 1917.

*The Green Cockatoo, and Other Plays*. Chicago: A. C. McClurg, 1913.

*Living Hours: Four One-Act Plays*. Boston: Badger, 1913.

*The Lonely Way. Intermezzo, Countess Mizzie. Three Plays*. Boston: Little, Brown, 1922.

*Reigen, The Affairs of Anatol, and Other Plays*. New York: The Modern Library, 1933.

## English Translations of Nondramatic Works

*Beatrice: A Novel.* New York: Simon & Schuster, 1926.

*Bertha Garlan.* Boston: Badger, 1913; and New York: Boni & Liveright, 1918.

"The Blind Geronimo and His Brother." In *German Stories: Deutsche Novellen*, pp. 189–239. Edited by Harry Steinhauer. New York: Bantam Books, 1961.

*Casanova's Homecoming.* New York: Thomas Seltzer, 1922; New York: Simon & Schuster, 1930; and New York: Avon, 1948.

*Daybreak.* New York: Simon & Schuster, 1927.

*Dr. Graesler.* New York: Thomas Seltzer, 1923; and New York: Simon & Schuster, 1930.

*Flight into Darkness.* New York: Simon & Schuster, 1931.

*Fräulein Else: A Novel.* New York: Simon & Schuster, 1925.

*The Mind in Words and Actions: Preliminary Remarks Concerning Two Diagrams.* New York: Frederick Ungar, 1972.

*My Youth in Vienna.* New York: Holt, Rinehart and Winston, 1970.

*None but the Brave* (Leutnant Gustl). New York: Simon & Schuster, 1926.

*Rhapsody: A Dream Novel.* New York: Simon & Schuster, 1927.

*The Road to the Open.* New York: Alfred A. Knopf, 1923.

*Some Day Peace Will Return: Notes on War and Peace.*
New York: Frederick Ungar, 1972.
*Theresa: The Chronicle of a Woman's Life.* New York:
Simon & Schuster, 1928.

COLLECTIONS

*Beatrice, and Other Stories.* London: T. Werner Laurie,
1926.
*Little Novels.* New York: Simon & Schuster, 1929.
*The Shepherd's Pipe, and Other Stories.* New York:
Nicholas L. Brown, 1922.
*Viennese Idylls.* Boston, John W. Luce, 1913.
*Viennese Novelettes.* New York: Simon & Schuster, 1931.

# Works about Schnitzler

Allen, Richard H. *An Annotated Arthur Schnitzler Bibli-
ography.* Chapel Hill: The University of North Caro-
lina Press, 1966. Additions to the above by Reinhard
Urbach. *Literatur und Kritik* 15 (June 1967):324–28.
Bailey, Joseph W. "Arthur Schnitzler's Dramatic Work."
*Texas Review* 5, no. 4 (July 1920):294–307.
Beharriell, Frederick J. "Arthur Schnitzler's Range of
Theme." *Monatshefte für deutschen Unterricht* 43, no.
7 (November 1951):301–311.
Bentley, Eric. *The Playwright as Thinker: A Study of
Drama in Modern Times*, pp. 263–64. New York: Har-
court, Brace, 1951.

Bithell, Jethro. *Modern German Literature 1880–1950*, pp. 229–37. London: Methuen, 1959.

Kann, Robert A. "Schnitzler as an Austrian Writer in the World Today." *Journal of the International Arthur Schnitzler Research Association* 1, nos. 4–5 (Autumn–Winter 1962):3–4.

Politzer, Heinz. "Arthur Schnitzler: Poetry of Psychology." *Modern Language Notes* 78, no. 4 (October 1963):353–72.

Reichert, Herbert W. "Arthur Schnitzler and Modern Ethics." *Journal of the International Arthur Schnitzler Research Association* 2, no. 1 (Spring 1963):21–24.

Reik, Theodor. *Arthur Schnitzler als Psycholog*. Minden, Westfalen: J. C. C. Bruns, 1913.

Seidlin, Oskar. "In Memoriam Arthur Schnitzler: May 15, 1862–Oct. 21, 1931." *American-German Review* 28, no. 4 (April–May 1962):4–6.

Specht, Richard. *Arthur Schnitzler: Der Dichter und sein Werk. Eine Studie*. Berlin: S. Fischer, 1922.

# INDEX